Contents

For my mother Grace—the amazing woman who raised six children
and taught us to find meaning in every ordinary moment.
Both you and Dad showed us strength when things got tough,
your kindness became our inspiration, your wisdom our guide.
This book exists because you taught us to listen,
to find the lessons hiding in plain sight.
*Every word is a thank you for showing us how to live with **grace**.*
I love you Mom.
It's going to be a good day!

Sometimes,
It's the ordinary
unintentional moments of
kindness, that mean the
most.

1

Because of the deer

S taff Sergeant Russell Smith checked his watch for the third time in ten minutes. The morning fog hung thick over the winding English countryside road as Private First Class Thompson navigated their Jeep toward the port. In the back seat, Colonel Barrett drummed his fingers impatiently against his leather briefcase.

"How much longer, Private?" the Colonel asked, his voice tight with concern. Their transport ship to France was scheduled to depart in less than an hour.

"Should be just around this bend, sir," Thompson replied, his young face tense with concentration. At twenty years old, he was still trying to prove himself worthy of such important assignments.

That's when they saw it - a young deer, seemingly materializing from the mist. Its wide eyes caught the Jeep's headlights, and for a moment, time stood still. Thompson swerved instinctively, but it was too late. The impact wasn't hard, but it was enough to send their Jeep into a shallow ditch.

The deer, merely stunned, scrambled to its feet and disappeared into the woods. The three men weren't so lucky. The Jeep's front axle was damaged, and by the time another vehicle could be dispatched to retrieve them, their ship, the HMS Victoria, had already departed.

Colonel Barrett was furious. Staff Sergeant Smith watched the ship disappear over the horizon, his stomach tight with anxiety about the delay in their deployment. Only young Thompson seemed affected by the deer itself, his face pale as he worried about both the animal and his career.

Three days later, the news reached their base. The HMS Victoria had been hit by a German U-boat in the English Channel. There were no survivors.

***

"And that's why you're here today, sweetheart," Russell Smith, now ninety-eight years old, told his great-granddaughter as they sat in his garden. The young girl's eyes were wide as she held his weathered hand.

"Because of a deer?" she asked, amazed.

Russell nodded, his eyes bright with tears and gratitude. "Because of a deer, I got to meet your great-grandmother. I got to raise your grandfather. I got to hold you when you were born." He gestured to the beautiful garden around them, filled with roses his wife had planted decades ago. "I got to live a life so full of love it sometimes feels like my heart might burst."

He leaned back in his chair, remembering that foggy morning in 1944. "You know, that young Private Thompson - he carried the guilt of that accident for weeks until we learned about the ship. After that, he lived every day like it was a gift. Became one of my closest friends. And, he went on to become a wildlife veterinarian after the war."

Russell picked up a photo from the small table beside him - a black and white image of three young men in uniform, arms around each other's shoulders, smiling despite the weight of war around them. "Colonel Barrett made it home on the next transport. He told me once that the deer saved him from his own ambition - taught him to slow down, appreciate the small moments."

His great-granddaughter squeezed his hand. "Do you think the deer knew?"

Russell chuckled softly. "I think life has a way of putting us exactly where we need to be, even when we don't understand it at the time." He looked out over his garden, where his family was gathering for Sunday dinner - four generations of lives that existed because of a deer on a foggy English morning.

"Sometimes the biggest blessings come disguised as accidents or mistakes," he continued. "The trick is to remember that every day above ground is a gift, every moment with family is precious, and every setback might just be life's way of steering us toward something wonderful."

The sound of laughter drifted over from the patio where his children and grandchildren were setting up for dinner. Russell smiled, feeling that familiar surge of gratitude that had become as much a part of him as breathing.

"You know what I think?" he said, his voice soft with emotion. "I think that deer was right on time."

> "Life can only be understood backwards; but it must be lived forwards." Søren Kierkegaard (1813-1855)

This story is inspired by the incredible true experience of my husband's father, James Russell Smith. A World War II veteran who fought in the Battle of the Bulge, his life was miraculously spared when he missed boarding a transport ship that later sank with no survivors.

***

Embrace the Good Day!

Remember, it's going to be a good day! Remember that the possibility of a good day is always within reach. It's a choice we make, a mindset we cultivate. We're all here together, sharing this journey, and each day is a precious gift. Let's choose to make it a good one, for ourselves and for others.

Three "It's Going to Be a Good Day" Ideas to Try:

1. Treat yourself to a small indulgence you don't normally allow, like a piece of chocolate or an afternoon nap.

2. Write down three things you're looking forward to this week, no matter how small.

3. Call someone who always makes you laugh and share a memory that brings you both joy, letting their positive energy brighten your outlook.

Today's Reflections:

In every challenge lies an invitation to discover your own quiet strength and unexpected grace.

itsgoingtobeagoodday©

2
The last quilt square

Coleen stood in the back corner of the fabric store, surrounded by bolts of cotton prints and batting, holding twelve precious embroidered quilt squares in her hands as if they were made of gold. In a way, they were more valuable than any precious metal – they were the last pieces her mother Grace had ever quilted, created with trembling ninety-seven-year-old hands for her newest great-granddaughter, Violet.

"What would Mom use?" she muttered to herself, a habit she'd developed over years of shopping alone. Her fingers traced the precise stitching on the squares, each one a testament to her mother's dedication to her craft. For twenty-four great-grandchildren, Grace had created twenty-four unique quilts, each one a masterpiece of love and patience. But now, with her hands no longer steady enough to guide the needle, these twelve squares were all that remained of that tradition.

The fluorescent lights hummed overhead as Coleen wandered between the aisles, overwhelmed by the endless choices of thread, backing, and batting. Her mother would have known exactly what to select, would have understood instinctively how to bring these pieces together into something beautiful. But Coleen had never learned the intricacies of quilting – there had always been tomorrow, always been next time, always been Mom to do it.

"It sounds like you might need some help, dear."

The voice was gentle, warm like honey in tea. Coleen turned to find a petite elderly woman with silver hair and kind eyes looking up at her. She wore a hand-knit sweater in soft purple, and a delicate brooch shaped like a sewing needle adorned her collar.

"Oh, I..." Coleen's voice caught as she held up the squares. "These are the last ones my mother made. She's ninety-seven now, and her hands..." She didn't need to finish the sentence. The woman nodded, understanding written across her face.

"My name is Marilyn Rose," the woman said, touching Coleen's arm gently. "Are you in a hurry?"

Coleen thought of her husband waiting in the truck outside. "Well, my husband's waiting..."

Marilyn's eyes twinkled. "Let him wait, dear. Some things are more important than a few minutes in a parking lot." She smiled conspiratorially. "Now, tell me about who this quilt is for."

As they walked the aisles together, Coleen shared the story of baby Violet, of her mother Grace's twenty-four quilts for twenty-four great-grandchildren, of the tradition that seemed to be ending with these twelve squares. Marilyn listened, nodding, her expert hands selecting threads and fabrics as they talked.

"You see this violet-colored thread?" Marilyn held up a spool. "It's perfect for the backing stitch, and it'll be our little secret tribute to your granddaughter's name." She chuckled warmly. "I don't really have a life, you know, except for quilting. Been part of the local quilting society for thirty years now."

But Coleen could see that wasn't true – Marilyn's life was rich with the wisdom she shared, the kindness she spread, the knowledge she passed on. For over an hour, she guided Coleen through every step of what would be needed, explaining techniques with the patience of a born teacher, sharing little tricks that only decades of experience could provide.

"You'll want to press these seams open," she demonstrated with her hands, "it helps the quilt lie flatter. Your mother would have done it the same way." She reached into her purse and pulled out a small business card, decorated with a delicate quilted pattern. "Here's my number, dear. Call me if you get stuck. We quilters have to stick together."

As Coleen gathered her purchases, she felt tears welling in her eyes. "I don't know how to thank you," she said. "This means so much..."

Marilyn patted her hand. "No thanks needed. You know, someday, when little Violet is all grown up, she might look at this quilt and wonder about its story. She'll know about her great-grandmother Grace's loving stitches, of course. But she won't know about today – about a daughter's love that wouldn't let a tradition end, or about a stranger in a fabric store who took the time to help. And that's exactly as it should be. The best kindnesses are the ones that weave themselves invisibly into the fabric of our lives."

Years later, when Violet would wrap herself in the quilt, tracing the patterns with her fingers, she wouldn't know about the afternoon spent in the back of a fabric store. She wouldn't know about Marilyn Rose with her purple sweater and her generous heart. But she would feel the love – Grace's last stitches, Coleen's determination, and the kindness of a stranger, all wrapped up together in a warm embrace that would last for generations.

Some might say it was just a quilt, just an afternoon, just a chance meeting between strangers. But in the tapestry of life, it's these moments of connection, these small acts of kindness, that create the strongest threads. They remind us that even as we age, our knowledge becomes a gift we can share, our experience a light we can hold up for others who find themselves in familiar darkness. And sometimes, the most profound impact we can have is simply taking the time to help someone else continue a story that seemed about to end.

"In the gentle hands of strangers, we sometimes find the thread that connects our past to our future. Like a quilt, life's most beautiful patterns emerge when kindness is stitched into its very fabric."

* This short story was told to me by my sister Coleen in 2025 when her granddaughter Violent was born and she had twelve quilt squares from our mother. The helpful strangers real name was Marilyn Rose. Marilyn maybe you'll read this story someday and realize just how much your time and kindness that day meant to someone.

So, How About That Good Day?

You know, it really is going to be a good day – or at least, it can be! And hey, if this particular story didn't hit the spot, no worries. The beauty of it is, you get to decide what kind of day you're going to have. We're all in this together, making the most of each day we're given. And honestly, isn't a good day way better than a not-so-good one?

Three Ways to Make Today a "Good Day":

1. **Offer your knowledge freely** - Like Marilyn Rose did with her quilting expertise, share what you know with someone who needs it. Your lifetime of experience could be exactly what someone else needs today, whether it's teaching a skill, sharing wisdom, or simply listening with understanding.

2. **Connect generations through tradition** - Take time to preserve or continue a meaningful tradition. Teach a young person a skill from your generation, share family stories, or help someone continue a tradition that might otherwise be lost—just as Coleen worked to continue her mother's quilting legacy for baby Violet.

3. **Recognize the beauty in seemingly small encounters** - Be present in everyday moments with strangers. A simple conversation in a store, an offered helping hand, or a shared smile might seem insignificant, but like Marilyn's assistance with the quilt, these moments can become part of a beautiful tapestry that extends far beyond what we can see.

My Good Day Notes:

Kindness is the only currency that grows richer when you spend it freely, creating ripples that reach shores you'll never see.

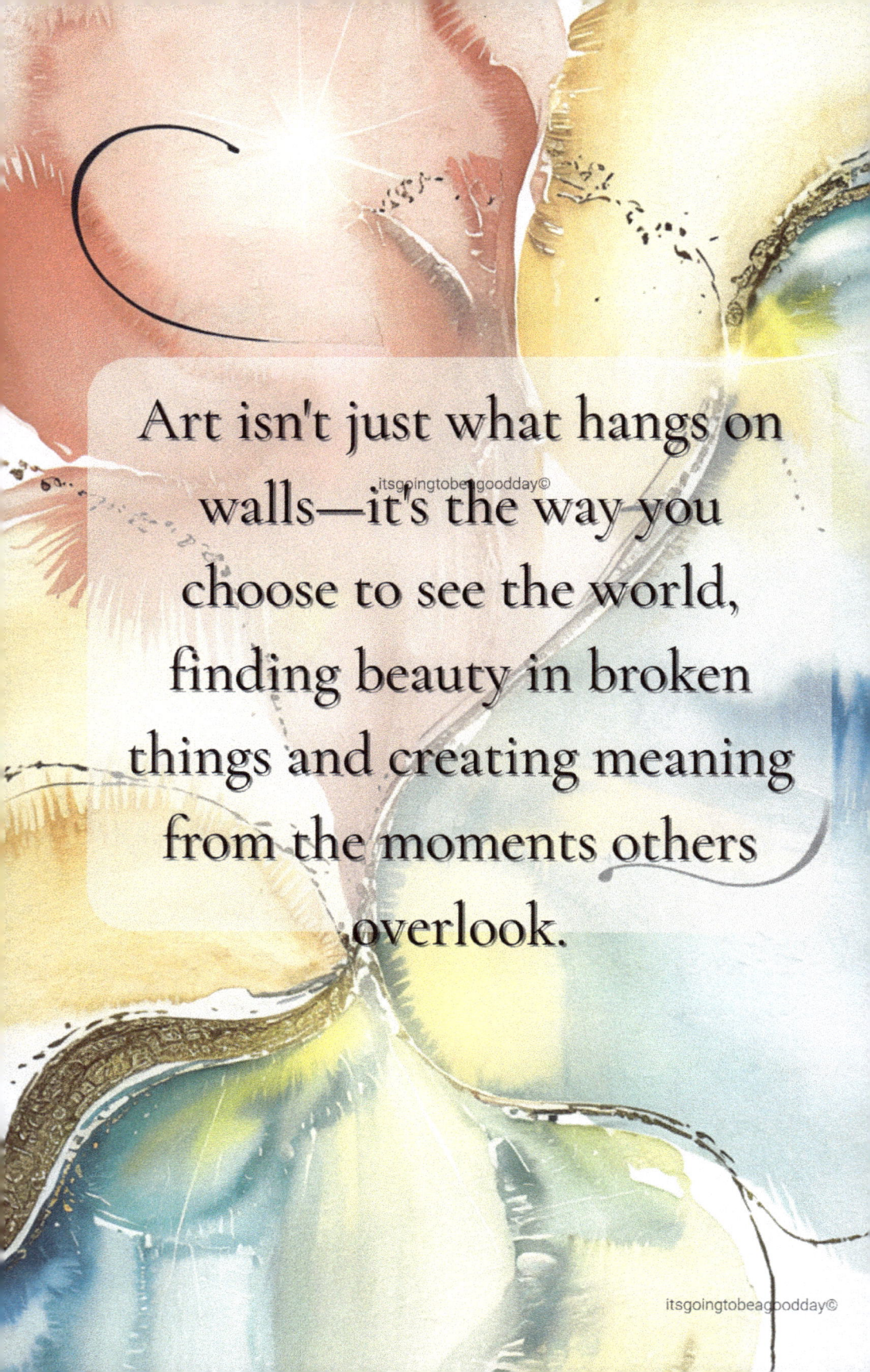

Art isn't just what hangs on walls—it's the way you choose to see the world, finding beauty in broken things and creating meaning from the moments others overlook.

itsgoingtobeagoodday©

3

The maple painter

The autumn wind, crisp and carrying the scent of woodsmoke and fallen leaves, ushered Arthur Grandas into Maplewood Assisted Living. He shuffled in, a cardigan draped over his shoulders like a resigned flag, his gaze fixed on the polished linoleum floor. Pennsylvania in autumn was a masterpiece of fiery hues, but Arthur felt only the graying edges of his own season.

His room was pleasant enough, overlooking a small garden where a solitary maple stood sentinel. Its leaves were a riot of scarlet and gold, defiant against the encroaching November chill.

"A fine view, Mr. Grandas," chirped a young aide with a sunshine smile, whose name tag read 'Bethany'.

Arthur just grunted, settling into the armchair. "I suppose it is." He unpacked his few belongings, each item a timestamp from his seventy-eight years of life—a career in accounting, a marriage that had ended too soon, children grown and scattered across the country.

Days melted into weeks. Arthur observed the other residents, a collage of wrinkles and whispers, each navigating their own version of twilight. He felt adrift, watching the vibrant world from a quiet harbor.

One afternoon, Bethany bounced into his room with unusual excitement. "Mr. Grandas, we have a special guest coming tomorrow—a local artist who's giving a demonstration. Everyone's talking about it!"

Arthur raised an eyebrow. "An artist? Here?"

"Dan Helsel," she said, eyes bright. "He's ninety-one and still painting! Isn't that wonderful?"

Arthur merely shrugged. "Good for him, I suppose."

The next day, curiosity got the better of him. Arthur joined the small crowd gathered in the community room, settling in the back row. A white-haired man with remarkably steady hands stood before an easel, with a box and a palette attached to it that held everything he needed to paint, and a canvas already bearing the beginnings of a landscape.

"I didn't touch a paintbrush for decades," Dan Helsel was saying, his voice surprisingly strong. "Last time I painted was 1965, the year my daughter Tracy was born. Then life happened—work, family, responsibilities."

Arthur found himself leaning forward.

"What changed?" someone asked.

Dan's eyes shone with warmth. "I retired at sixty. My wife Jane and I went to the National Gallery in Washington DC with Jane's sister and her husband, to see the Mona Lisa. The lines were enormous, snaking through several different galleries, When we entered the Dutch Masters Gallery, I was amazed to see how they painted, fabric, metal and glass and how they captured the light. While everyone rushed to see her famous smile, I found myself transfixed by paintings most people walked past."

As Dan spoke, his brush moved across the canvas, transforming blank space into a luminous landscape.

"Those still lifes, those landscapes... something stirred in me that day. Something I thought had died." He added a touch of golden light to the horizon. "The creative spirit inside you never dies. Sometimes it just needs the right moment to reawaken."

After the demonstration, while others crowded around Dan, Arthur slipped back to his room. He stood at his window, gazing at the maple tree, seeing it with new eyes. The way the light caught its leaves, the shadows it cast across the lawn—was this how an artist would see it?

A week later, Bethany entered Arthur's room with a small box tied with a cheerful yellow ribbon. Inside was a beginner's painting set with tubes promising colors with names like 'Crimson Glory' and 'Sky Azure'.

"I can't," Arthur protested. "I've never painted in my life."

"Mr. Helsel is coming back next month for a workshop," Bethany said. "He said it's never too late to start."

She set up the easel by the window, placed the canvas, and squeezed a dollop of crimson onto a plastic palette. "Just start somewhere," she encouraged. "Pick a color. Any color."

After she left, Arthur sat for a long time, just looking. The maple outside was now dusted with the first snow of winter, a delicate frosting on its bare branches. He picked up a brush, tentatively dipped it in the crimson, and touched it to the canvas. A small, hesitant stroke. It looked... inadequate.

But he continued, adding a daub of white, then a smear of grey. The act of applying paint, of seeing color bloom on the stark white canvas, was absorbing. His first attempt was clumsy, an abstract swirl of muted colors that vaguely suggested the tree outside.

When Dan's workshop arrived, Arthur brought his painting, embarrassed but determined. Dan examined it with kind eyes.

"Abstract expressionism," he nodded. "Very modern."

Arthur shook his head. "Just blobs. I was trying to paint the tree."

"Then let me show you how," Dan said, pulling up a chair beside him.

Under Dan's guidance, Arthur learned to see the tree differently—not just as a maple, but as shapes of light and shadow, as colors that shifted with the changing light. Dan shared stories of his own journey—how after that day at the National Gallery, he'd started with Bob Ross tutorials, only to discover they weren't what he wanted.

"I found my teacher, Jim Sulkowski, in Canonsburg, PA." Dan explained. "Drove hours each week for four years to learn the Old Masters style techniques. My wife Jane thought I was crazy—until I finished a painting she refused to let me sell."

Arthur smiled. "What did she say?"

"She took my brush, made a tiny brush stroke in the corner, and said, 'See? I helped paint that one.' She did that until the day she passed, but I know she still 'helps' with every painting."

Week by week, Arthur's skills grew. He learned to prepare canvases, to mix colors, to see the world through an artist's eyes. The maple tree remained his constant subject, its changing moods reflected in his growing portfolio.

When spring arrived, Arthur participated in the facility's first resident art show. His painting—the maple tree in winter dawn, light glinting off snow-laden branches—earned admiring comments.

Dan attended the exhibition, beaming like a proud father. "Not bad for a beginner," he teased.

Arthur grinned. "I had a good teacher."

"You had the spirit inside you all along," Dan countered. "I just helped you find it."

As summer bloomed, Arthur began teaching other residents. His room had become a studio, his life a canvas reimagined. Each morning, he greeted the maple tree like an old friend, noting the play of light through its leaves, the dance of shadows across the lawn. It's going to be a good day, he thought to himself, a new mantra that bubbled up inside automatically, everyday he picked up a paintbrush.

One year after arriving at Maplewood feeling like his story was ending, Arthur Grandas, now seventy-nine, discovered it was just taking an unexpected turn. When his daughter visited, astonished to find him before an easel, Arthur gestured to a small plaque beside his paintings:

"The creative spirit inside you never dies. Sometimes it just needs the right moment to reawaken." —inspired by Dan Helsel

*This story was inspired by Dan Helsel, a real-life artist who redis-covered his passion for painting after retirement. Beginning his artistic journey anew at age 60 after laying down his brushes in 1965, Dan studied under James Sulkowski at The Sulkowski Academy of Fine Art in Canonsburg, Pennsylvania. His landscape and still life paintings have been featured in exhibitions throughout western and central Penn-sylvania, earning numerous awards. Known for his technique reminis-cent of the Old Masters, Dan paints on oil-primed linen canvas and prepares his own panels using Renaissance formulas. At 91, he continues to paint today, having designed and patented the Dan Helsel Painters Palette Box used by artists throughout the country. To date Dan has painted over 500 oil paintings.

***

The Choice is Ours: A Good Day Awaits.

The promise of a good day is always present, a potential waiting to be realized. Whether this story resonated deeply or simply passed by, the underlying truth remains: each day is a canvas, and we are the artists. We hold the brush, and we choose the colors. Let's choose to paint a good day, a masterpiece of small joys and meaningful moments.

Three Brushstrokes for a Good Day:

1. Choose one subject to observe daily through changing seasons, just as Arthur did with his maple tree, and let it teach you to seethe world differently.

2. "The creative spirit inside you never dies" – pick up that paintbrush, pen, or instrument you've always wanted to try, regardless of your age. Try a new craft or perhaps an adult paint-by-number.

3. Share your newfound passion with others, creating your own ripple effect of inspiration, like Arthur did when he began teaching fellow residents.

Reflections on my Canvas of Today:

Dan Helsel

The light you're searching for has always lived within you—sometimes it just needs your permission to shine

4
Captain's wisdom

Morgan slammed her bedroom door, threw her backpack across the room, and collapsed onto her bed. Her phone buzzed—Dad calling. With a dramatic sigh, she answered.

"This is literally the worst day ever," she moaned before her father could speak. "Cassie told everyone about what happened at Emily's party, and now the whole school is talking about it. And they just canceled 'Riverview High'! The one T.V. show that actually gets me. I can't even."

"Honey, I'm sorry," her father said. "But it's not the end—"

"You don't understand," Morgan interrupted. "My life is over. Everything is ruined."

After hanging up, Morgan buried her face in her pillow. A gentle knock at the door made her groan.

"Go away, Mom," she called out to her mother.

The door opened anyway, and Dana peeked in. "Bad day?"

"The worst."

Dana sat on the edge of the bed, reaching out to stroke Morgan's hair. "Want to talk about it?"

Morgan repeated her litany of disasters while Dana listened patiently. When Morgan finally paused for breath, Dana said, "Kurt will be home soon. Maybe talking to him will help."

"Kurt doesn't care about my problems," Morgan mumbled into her pillow.

"That's not true," Dana said softly. "He cares more than you know."

***

When Morgan's stepfather, Kurt, arrived home, the smell of dinner cooking lured Morgan downstairs. She slumped at the kitchen table, scrolling through social media and ignoring her parents' conversation.

"Someone had a rough day," Dana whispered to Kurt, nodding toward Morgan.

Kurt, still in his Coast Guard uniform, studied his daughter. The lines around his eyes deepened.

"How was school?" he asked, sitting across from Morgan.

"Terrible," she muttered without looking up.

"Want to tell me about it?"

Morgan sighed dramatically and launched into her tale of woe again—the betrayal, the canceled show, the unfairness of it all.

Kurt listened quietly, his weathered hands wrapped around a mug of coffee. When Morgan finished with, "So yeah, worst day ever," he remained silent for a long moment.

"Do you really want to know what I think?" he finally asked.

Morgan rolled her eyes. "Sure, Kurt."

"You're not having a bad day," he said simply.

Morgan's head snapped up. "What? Were you even listening?"

"I was," he said. "And I'm telling you, what you're experiencing isn't a bad day."

"Then what is it?" Morgan asked, defensive and confused.

Kurt set down his coffee. "Twenty years ago, I was Captain Morgan," he said with the hint of a sad smile. "Different Morgan, but that's what the crew called me. I commanded a crab fishing vessel in the Bering Sea—hundred-ton boat, crew of thirty-two. Brutal work, dangerous conditions."

Morgan had heard bits of her stepfather's past life, but he rarely spoke about his time as a Captain or as a fisherman.

"One winter day, another boat radioed in, asking where the catch was good. I told them about a spot we'd just left—plenty of crab, but a storm system was moving in fast. I warned them to be careful."

Kurt's voice grew quieter. "They found the crab all right. Started pulling in more than they should have, stayed too long despite the weather warnings. When the storm hit, it hit hard. Waves over thirty feet. Their boat capsized."

He looked directly at Morgan, his eyes holding the weight of memory.

"Nine men died that day, eight survived. We were the closest vessel, but by the time we reached them..." He shook his head. "The sea was too rough. We couldn't save them all."

Morgan sat frozen, her phone forgotten on the table.

"That was a bad day, Morgan. Watching men die because someone made a poor decision, and not being able to do anything about it—that's a bad day."

He reached across the table and placed his hand over hers.

"What you're going through feels important right now, and your feelings are valid. But perspective matters. Tomorrow, Cassie's gossip will be old news. Another show will come along. But those nine families? They never got their loved ones back."

Morgan's eyes filled with tears. "I didn't know," she whispered.

"I don't tell that story often," Kurt said. "But sometimes we need reminders of what truly matters. The day you're having? It's actually going to be a good day—because you're here, you're safe, and you have people who love you."

Morgan stood and walked around the table, wrapping her arms around her step-father's neck. "I'm sorry."

He patted her arm. "Don't be sorry. Just be grateful. Each morning, tell yourself: 'It's going to be a good day.' Because any day you get to keep living is a good day."

As they sat down to dinner, Morgan looked at her family with new eyes. Her stepfather's words echoed in her mind, and she silently made a promise to herself: she would remember the nine men who never came home, and she would try, every day, to maintain perspective.

"The happiest people don't have the best of everything, they just make the best of everything they have." – Anonymous

Inspired by the real Captain Morgan, who sadly witnessed nine men die one day in the sea. Captain did tell the story to his stepdaughter when she thought she was having the worst day ever.

Three Ways to Have a Good Day:

1. Begin with gratitude for what you have, not resentment for what you don't.

2. Measure your troubles against true tragedy to maintain perspective.

3. Remember that you are writing your story each day—make it one worth telling.

Behind every face you pass lives an entire universe of hopes, memories, and quiet courage.

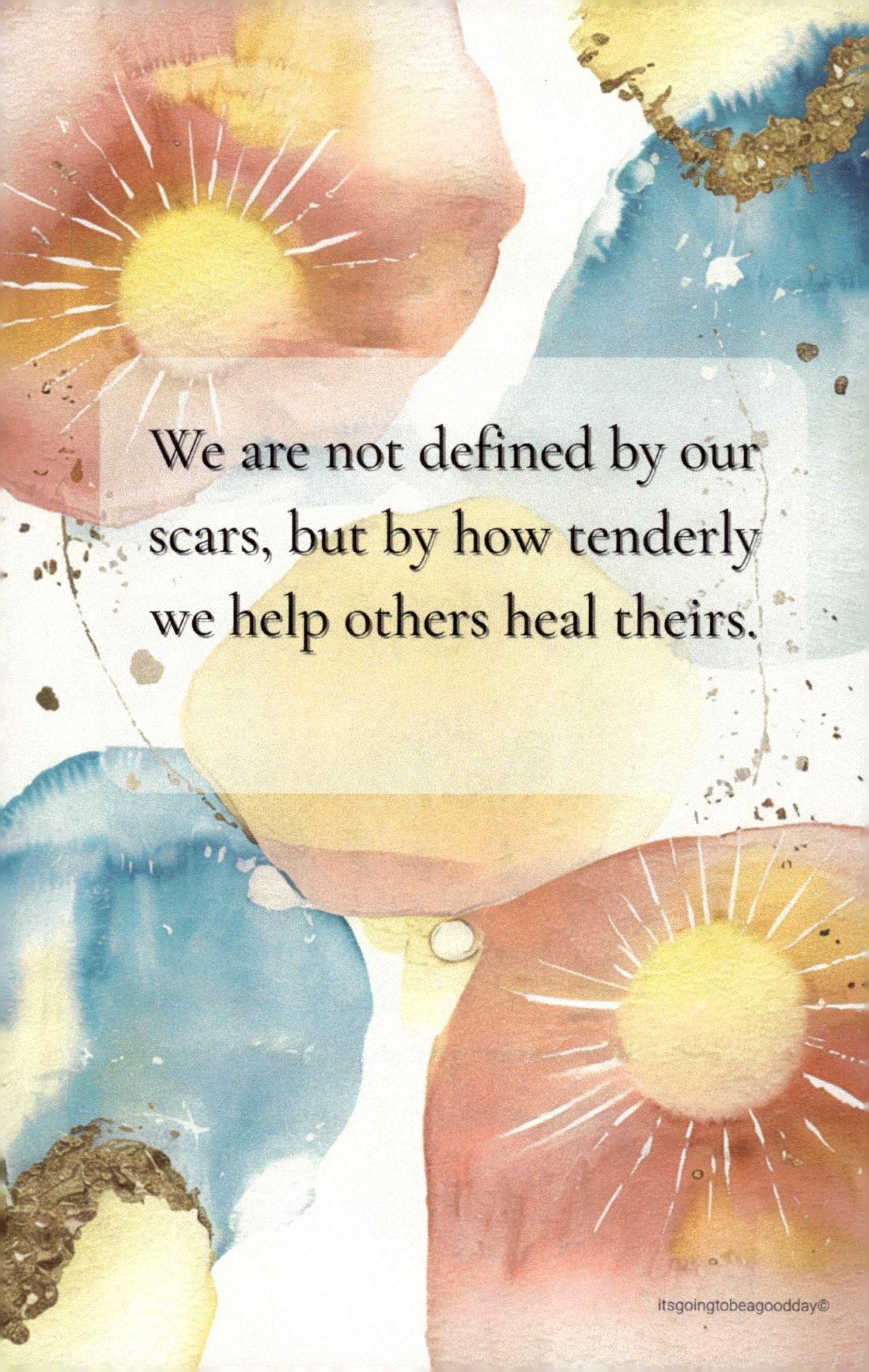

We are not defined by our scars, but by how tenderly we help others heal theirs.

5

3 o'clock in the morning

Dad always said he wanted his funeral at three o'clock in the morning. "That's when you'll know who your real friends are," he'd declare with that mischievous twinkle in his eye. "Who's gonna show up at three AM to say goodbye?"

It was the kind of thing that made perfect sense coming from him - a man who'd spent his life working impossible hours, first as a coal miner, then as a steel worker, somehow finding time to run a hotel bar with his brother between shifts. He lived life on his own schedule, and apparently, he planned to leave it the same way.

I never heard this story while he was alive. Being the youngest of six children, there were probably a lot of Dad's stories I missed. It wasn't until we were all gathered at Mom's house, preparing for the funeral, that she shared it with my brother. We were sitting around the kitchen table, that familiar gathering spot where so many family stories had been told over the years, when Mom mentioned Dad's unusual funeral request.

In that moment, surrounded by my siblings, all of us wrestling with our grief in different ways, something about that story lodged in my heart. Maybe it was because it was so perfectly Dad - practical and funny and a little bit contrary, just like he'd always been. Or maybe it was because in the midst of our loss, it gave us something to smile about.

That night, unable to sleep and feeling that particular kind of restlessness that comes with grief, I convinced my sister and a few friends to honor

Dad's wish - at least in spirit. The Polish Falcons club was technically supposed to close at 2 AM, like all bars in Pennsylvania, but the bartender - the mother of my high school friend - understood something about grief and memory and love. She kept the lights on for us.

We called everyone we could think of who knew Dad, and by three o'clock in the morning, we had assembled a small but dedicated group. We raised our glasses to a man who'd spent his life working hard, loving deeply, and occasionally suggesting impossible funeral times.

Afterward, my sister and I took a detour to the cemetery. It was one of those perfect Pennsylvania nights - clear and star-filled, as if the universe itself was keeping watch. We stood there under that vast sky, saying the things you say to fathers who leave too soon, each of us having our own private conversation with the stars.

The next afternoon at the funeral, the sky opened up. The kind of rain that soaks through umbrellas and makes people huddle under funeral tent awnings, their shoes sinking into the wet grass. As we stood there, getting steadily drenched, I could almost hear Dad's voice: "Well, it wasn't raining at three o'clock in the morning, was it?"

That's the thing about final requests - they're not really about the request at all. Dad's three AM funeral wasn't about testing who would show up. It was about who he was - a man who worked the odd hours, who knew the value of true friendship, who could find humor in the darkest places. It was about the stories we tell and retell, the way we keep people alive in our memories.

Now, years later, whenever I'm awake at three in the morning - maybe jet-lagged from traveling between time zones, or up late with my own thoughts - I think about Dad. I think about that night at the Polish Falcons, about stars and rain and siblings and grief. I think about how sometimes the hardest moments create the most lasting memories, how laughter and tears aren't opposites but partners in the dance of remembrance.

And I've decided to carry on the tradition. I've told my own siblings, husband and friends that when my time comes, I want my funeral at three o'clock in the morning - though I haven't specified which time zone. Let them figure that out. After all, the best family stories always leave a little room for interpretation.

Because sometimes the most meaningful way to honor someone's memory isn't just to remember what they said, but to keep their spirit alive in the way they would have appreciated most - even if that means raising a glass at an impossible hour, sharing stories under the stars, or planning your own unreasonable funeral requests.

Dad would have liked that. He might have even shown up - at exactly three AM, just to prove a point.

"To live in hearts we leave behind is not to die" Thomas Campbell, a Scottish poet (1777-1844).

Inspired by my father Peter C. Kaltenbaugh Sr. who really did say that he wanted to be buried at 3 o'clock in the morning. As he stated, "...that's how you'll know who your friends and family really are."

Ready for a Good Day?

It's going to be a good day – but what will you do to make it so? Did this story spark any ideas? Even if it didn't, remember that every day offers a fresh start, a new opportunity to create something positive. We're all here, living this life together, and we have the power to shape our days.

Three "It's Going to Be a Good Day" Ideas to Try:

1. Share a story about a parent with someone today.

2. Call a friend or family member you haven't spoken with in a while and share one happy memory that makes you both smile.

3. Reach out to someone younger than you and ask what brings them joy these days—their answer might introduce you to something new worth trying.

The most profound transformations happen in moments so gentle they're almost missed.

6

The flower in the crack

Every morning, Julene walked past the same stretch of cracked concrete on her way to work. It was an unremarkable spot - just another broken piece of sidewalk in the city. But one spring morning, she noticed something different: a tiny green shoot pushing its way through one of the cracks.

Most people hurried past without a second glance, but Julene found herself pausing. There was something compelling about this small sign of life emerging from such an unlikely place. The next day, she left home a few minutes earlier so she could stop and check on the plant's progress.

Days turned into weeks, and Julene's morning ritual became sacred. She'd bring a little water in a bottle when the weather was dry, and sometimes she'd talk to the plant in soft whispers. Her coworkers thought she was crazy when she mentioned her daily visits, but Julene didn't mind. She saw something they didn't - the quiet determination of life finding its way toward the light.

The stem grew stronger, pushing up through the narrow space despite the odds. When the first bud appeared, Julene could hardly contain her excitement. She decided to name it Violet. She had a favorite Aunt that had passed away when she was young and her name was Aunt Violet, a strong and courageous woman who battled a stressful year, during the war when her husband went missing.

Now that it had a name, she had even more reason for this resilient plant to grow. She didn't know why she was so attached to the plant, but it was simply that, she was. She wondered what kind of flower it would become. Would it be a common dandelion, a beautiful violet or perhaps a stubborn weed? But something told her to keep watching, to keep believing.

Then one morning, just as the sun was rising, Julene arrived to find the bud had opened. There, emerging from the crack in the concrete, was the most magnificent iris she had ever seen. Its petals were a deep, iridescent purple with delicate white streaks, like brush strokes painted by an artist. The flower seemed to glow in the early morning light, its beauty made even more striking by its humble surroundings.

Julene sat on a nearby bench, tears welling in her eyes. She thought about all the mornings she'd spent watching this flower grow, all the times she could have walked past like everyone else. Instead, she had witnessed something extraordinary - not just the bloom itself, but the entire journey from that first tiny shoot to this moment of perfect beauty.

From that day forward, Julene never again doubted that beauty could emerge from broken places, or that patience and attention could reveal everyday miracles. She learned that the most remarkable things often happen in the most unremarkable spaces, and that sometimes, all it takes is the willingness to stop and notice.

Years later, when people asked about the small iris tattoo on her wrist, Julene would smile and tell them about the flower that grew through the crack in the concrete, and how it taught her that hope can bloom anywhere - you just have to be willing to watch it grow.

Don't ever give up hope.

"Keep your face always toward the sunshine—and shadows will fall behind you." - Walt Whitman (American poet, 1819-1892)

*This story was inspired by a co-worker at Western Maryland College in 1994.

***

It's Going to Be a Good Day – Make It Happen!

As the title says, it is going to be a good day. And if this story didn't bring a smile, a chuckle, or a moment of reflection, that's okay! The power to make today good is in your hands. We're all here on this Earth, and every day we get is a chance to choose joy, to choose kindness, to choose to make it a good one. It's always a better choice than the alternative!

Three "It's Going to Be a Good Day" Ideas to Try:

1. Plant a seed in a small pot and place it where you'll see it daily, letting it remind you that growth takes time and consistent care.

2. Rearrange one small area of your home, like a shelf or tabletop, to give yourself a fresh perspective.

3. Move a chair to face a different direction in your home, giving yourself a completely new perspective of a familiar space.

You don't have to move mountains today—sometimes tending your own garden with love creates the most profound change.

We rise by lifting others; we shine by igniting the light in those around us.

7
Letters through time

Time has a way of folding in on itself, of bringing the past and present together in unexpected moments that take our breath away. For Megan, these moments lived in a box of yellowed letters, each one carefully preserved by her grandmother Barbara Jeanne – precious paper vessels carrying words of love across decades.

As a young girl, Megan had always been drawn to the stories of her grandparents. When both had passed on, leaving behind their earthly possessions, she had asked for just one thing: the letters her grandfather Russell had written during World War II. Every single day of his service, without fail, he had penned his thoughts to his beloved Barbara Jeanne, each letter a testament to a love that refused to bow to distance or circumstance.

"My dearest Barbara Jeanne," they would begin, and in them, he poured out his heart about their daughters, their future, their country, and most of all, his fervent desire to return home to her arms. Each one ended the same way – XXXOOO followed by three playful scribbles, a signature as unique as their love story.

In those days, letter writing was an art form, a daily ritual that connected hearts across oceans. Today's world of instant messages, emails, and video calls has made communication easier, but perhaps something precious has been lost in the rush of pixels and digital words. There's a permanence to ink on paper, a tangible connection that no amount of technological advancement can replicate. Even as artificial intelligence transforms how we interact, there's a growing appreciation for the simple power of hand-written words – each letter shaped by human emotion, each page holding the literal fingerprints of love.

For years, Megan kept these letters close, knowing somehow that they held something precious, something that transcended their paper and ink existence. As she grew into her artistic talents at Point Loma Nazarene University in California, the letters began to whisper to her of possibilities, of ways to bridge the gap between then and now, between memory and moment.

And so began her masterpiece.

On the day of her thesis presentation, family members gathered from across the country, curious about what Megan had created. Among them was her Uncle David, Russell and Barbara Jeanne's youngest child – one who hadn't even been a dream in those wartime letters, born in the peaceful years that followed. He came with his wife, Carrie, both of them eager to see how their niece had chosen to honor the family's history.

The exhibition space was filled with impressive works –sculptures reaching toward the ceiling, paintings that caught the eye and held it. But Megan's installation waited in its own space, separated from the rest by a simple doorway into darkness.

The first thing visitors heard was the steady tick-tick-tick of a metronome, marking time with the same relentless precision that had measured the days Russell spent away from Barbara Jeanne. As eyes adjusted to the dim light, the walls came alive – every surface covered with those precious letters, their words of love and longing creating a tapestry of memory and emotion.

Above, projected on the ceiling, modern moments flowed one into another – photographs Megan had taken in Greece, capturing every minute of a single day. Twenty-four hours of present-day life playing out above the written testament of past love. The effect was mesmerizing, a visual representation of how time is both linear and circular, how moments stack upon moments until they create the fabric of our lives.

Standing there, David studied one of his father's letters, a smile playing at his lips as he noticed the familiar XXXOOO and those three mysterious scribbles at the bottom. Carrie, watching her husband's face soften with memory, pointed to the signature.

"What are those squiggles after the X's and O's?" she asked, curious about this piece of family history she had married into.

David laughed softly, a knowing glint in his eye that reminded her so much of Russell. "Well, you know," was all he said, and in that moment, Carrie couldn't help but laugh too. The apple indeed hadn't fallen far from the tree, even for the son who came after the letters had stopped.

In that dark room, with the metronome keeping time and memories flowing all around them, visitors found themselves transported. Some wiped away quiet tears as they read Russell's words of devotion. Others stood transfixed by the interplay of past and present overhead. Each person who entered left changed, carrying with them a deeper understanding of how love echoes through time.

Perhaps that's why letter writing seems to be experiencing a quiet renaissance in our digital age. Young people, tired of the brief nature of texts and social media posts, are rediscovering the joy of putting pen to paper. They're learning what Russell and Barbara Jeanne knew all those years ago – that there's something magical about taking the time to create a message by hand, about knowing that someone will hold these words and read them again and again, about creating something that might be discovered decades later by someone who needs to feel connected to love's enduring power.

Megan's installation did more than display old letters or showcase photographs – it created a space where time itself seemed to pause, where a grandfather's love for his wife could live alongside his granddaughter's artistic vision, where every tick of the metronome reminded visitors that while time moves forever forward, love and memory have the power to transcend its boundaries.

For in the end, that's what time really is – not just the steady march of seconds and minutes, but the beautiful collision of moments that shape our lives. It's young Russell writing to his beloved Barbara Jeanne, it's their youngest son David discovering his father's heart through yellowed pages, it's their granddaughter Megan bringing these treasures into the light, it's all of us standing in a darkened room, reminded that love, in all its forms, is the thread that stitches time together.

And sometimes, if we're lucky, we get to see all those moments at once, brought together by something as simple as a box of old letters and the creative vision of a granddaughter who understood that the greatest art comes from the heart, signed with love and three mysterious scribbles that mean exactly what you think they mean.

> "Time flies over us, but leaves its shadow behind." - Nathaniel Hawthorne (1804-1864)

---

* This beautiful story was inspired by my niece Megan who is an artist, an illustrator, and a loving wife and mother. This was her college project.

***

3 Things to do to make it a Good Day:

1. What can you do today to remember time's passage, which can be interpreted as memories, experiences, and the impact we have on others.

2. Sort through old photographs for fifteen minutes and allow yourself to remember one beautiful moment.

3. Write a short note of gratitude to someone who helped you recently, even in a small way. Mail it snail mail, old school style! who knows who might read it ...one day in the future.

Write a short list of people who you would like to write an old fashioned letter to, then just do it!

itsgoingtobeagoodday©

The light you're searching for has always lived within you—sometimes it just needs your permission to shine

8

Heart of a champion

J.R. Barrett stood at the edge of the football field, his cleats digging into the familiar Arizona dirt as the setting sun painted the sky in brilliant oranges and reds. At five-foot-eight-and-a-half and 145 pounds, he wasn't the towering figure most college recruiters sought, but beneath his modest frame beat the heart of a giant. His high school career had been nothing short of remarkable – breaking local records, leading his team to victory after victory, and earning the respect of teammates who towered over him.

When the call came from the prestigious New Mexico Military Institute, the same institution that had produced legendary quarterback Roger Staubach, J.R.'s heart soared. This was his chance, his shot at proving that determination could overcome any physical limitation. The thirteen-hour drive from Arizona felt like a journey toward destiny, each mile bringing him closer to his dream.

But dreams, as J.R. would learn, sometimes crash against the hard wall of reality. The coach's dismissive laugh still echoed in his ears as he and his family left the office that day. "Too small for a scholarship," the coach had said, barely glancing at the game tapes that showed J.R.'s exceptional performance on the field. "It was a waste of time driving all this way."

That evening, in a quiet hotel room, J.R.'s father found him sitting on the bed, shoulders slumped, the weight of rejection pressing down on him like a heavy tackle. He sat beside him, his voice gentle but firm. "J.R., you have two options," he said, taking his hand. "You can be defeated, mope around, and say you weren't good enough. Or you can go home, build your strength, work harder than anyone else, and come back to show that coach what he missed. Those are your options. Pick one."

In that moment, something shifted in J.R.'s eyes. The defeat gave way to determination, and he made his choice. The next months became a testimony to human willpower. Every morning before dawn, he was in the weight room. Every afternoon, he ran drills until his legs burned. Every meal was calculated to add muscle to his frame. His body transformed, but more importantly, his spirit hardened into unbreakable steel.

When J.R. returned to the Military Institute, he wasn't asking for a scholarship anymore – he had already been accepted academically. This time, he was there to walk on to the team, to earn his place through sheer force of will. The same coach who had laughed him out of the office months before now watched in growing amazement as J.R. (now 195 pounds of muscle) outperformed player after player in training.

From a small locker at the end of the row, J.R. built his legacy. Within a week, he had earned a spot on the traveling team. Game after game, he proved that heart couldn't be measured in inches or pounds. His name began appearing in record books, and eventually, it found its place on the wall of honor, right beneath Roger Staubach's – a testament to the power of perseverance.

The coach, humbled by J.R.'s journey, later admitted that the experience changed how he evaluated players forever. He learned that champions aren't always cut from the same cloth, that greatness sometimes comes in unexpected packages. J.R.'s story became a legend at the institution, not just for his athletic achievements, but for the lesson it taught: never judge a dream by the size of the dreamer.

Today, J.R.'s story resonates far beyond the football field. It speaks to anyone who's ever been told they're too old, too small, too different, or too anything to achieve their dreams. It reminds us that life always presents us with two options: we can accept the limitations others place on us, or we can work to prove them wrong.

For those in their golden years wondering if it's too late to start a new chapter, J.R.'s story whispers, "It's never too late." For retirees questioning their purpose, it declares, "Your next great achievement awaits." Like Thomas Edison, who failed thousands of times before illuminating the world, J.R. shows us that persistence isn't just about reaching a goal – it's about becoming someone stronger in the pursuit.

As J.R.'s name continues to shine on that wall in New Mexico, it serves as a beacon for dreamers of all ages. It reminds us that our potential isn't measured by others' expectations, but by our willingness to rise after each fall, to push beyond our comfort zones, and to believe in ourselves when no one else will. Because in the end, the size of our success isn't determined by physical stature or age, but by the size of our heart and the strength of our determination.

J.R.'s legacy teaches us that every morning brings two options: we can let our dreams fade with yesterday's disappointments, or we can lace up our boots and step onto our own field of possibilities, ready to prove that our greatest chapters may still lie ahead. The choice, as always, is ours to make.

"If it's gonna be, it's up to me!"

Inspired by the true life college experience of J.R.

***

Turning the Page to a Good Day.

Every story has an ending, but every day is a new beginning. Maybe this story resonated with you, maybe it didn't. But the beauty of life is that we get to keep turning the page, keep exploring, keep finding the good. And today? Today has all the potential to be a truly good day. Let's embrace it.

Three Ways to help make today a Good Day:

1. Before bed, think of three positive things that happened today, no matter how small they seemed.

2. Try a new route on your daily walk, even if it's just turning left instead of right.

3. Write a short note of encouragement to your younger self, then apply that same compassionate advice to a challenge you're facing today.

J.R.

Sometimes a single kind word holds enough power to illuminate someone's darkest day.

9
What we carry

J udy Wallace had a ritual. Every morning at precisely seven-thirty, she laced up her walking shoes, tucked her house key into her pocket, and set out for her daily four-mile walk through the winding streets of Oakwood Heights. After thirty years of teaching elementary school, retirement had gifted her with mornings that belonged entirely to herself. These walks were sacred—a time to clear her mind, observe the changing seasons, and occasionally, to witness the small dramas of everyday life unfolding in her community.

It was during one such walk on a crisp autumn Tuesday that Judy deviated from her usual route. A detour sign for road construction had forced her down Sycamore Lane, a street she rarely visited. The universe, it seemed, had plans for her that morning.

As she rounded the corner, Judy noticed a specialized transport bus for persons with disabilities pulling up to a modest blue house with white trim. The front yard was already cluttered with packages of various sizes—some in brown cardboard, others in padded envelopes. The bus lowered its platform, and a young woman emerged.

The woman appeared to be in her mid-twenties, with dark hair pulled back in a messy ponytail. She wore a purple sweater that hung loosely on her thin frame. Her movements were somewhat hesitant, and she had the distinctive features that Judy recognized from her years of teaching as indicative of Down syndrome. What captured Judy's attention, however, was the look of overwhelm on the young woman's face as she surveyed the collection of packages awaiting her.

Judy slowed her pace, watching as the young woman signed something for the driver before attempting to gather the packages. Her arms were already laden with several bags she'd brought with her on the bus. She tried to balance the new packages precariously, managing to lift three before they tumbled from her grasp onto the grass. A soft sound of frustration carried across the lawn.

The bus remained idling at the curb, its driver watching through the large windshield. Judy hesitated. Should she intervene? She wasn't one to intrude on strangers' business, but something about the young woman's repeated attempts—picking up packages only to have them fall again—tugged at her heart.

Just as Judy was about to cross the street to offer assistance, another vehicle pulled up behind the bus. A silver truck with a "Happy Hands Cleaning Service" logo on the door. A woman in her sixties with blonde-colored hair jumped out, her movements quick and decisive.

"Need some help with those?" the newcomer called out, approaching the young woman with a friendly wave.

Judy paused, watching the interaction unfold. The young woman looked up, relief washing over her features.

"I'm Iris," the blonde-haired woman said, extending her hand. "I clean for Mrs. Thomas down the street. Saw you struggling with all this and thought you might need an extra pair of hands."

"Emily," the young woman replied, her voice soft but audible from where Judy stood. "Thank you. It's... it's a lot more than I expected."

Judy moved closer, not wanting to intrude but drawn to the unfolding scene of kindness. She positioned herself near a maple tree, its crimson leaves providing both beauty and cover.

"Let's get these inside," Iris said, already bending to collect the largest box. "One trip at a time is the only way to do it."

Emily nodded, visibly relieved. "The door's unlocked."

What followed was a methodical process of carrying packages inside, one by one. Iris chatted easily as they worked, her voice carrying in the morning air.

"So what's with all the packages? Early Christmas shopping?"

Emily shook her head as they emerged for another load. "Medical supplies, mostly. And some household items." Her voice dropped slightly. "My mom's coming home from the hospital soon. She's been there for almost three weeks."

"That's rough," Iris said, her tone softening. "Is it just you taking care of her?"

"Yeah," Emily replied, struggling with a particularly awkward box. "It's been that way since I was sixteen. Mom and I take care of each other."

Judy found herself holding her breath, listening to this glimpse into a stranger's life—a life of quiet challenges and enduring love.

As the women continued their work, Emily gradually opened up more. Judy couldn't hear every word, but she caught fragments about Emily's mother's recent pneumonia, complications with her condition, and Emily's fears about managing alone now that her mother's care needs had increased.

"I took off work to get everything ready," Emily explained as they carried in what appeared to be a medical bed rail. "The hospital social worker ordered all these supplies, but I didn't realize they'd all arrive at once."

"Do you work somewhere?" Iris asked, holding the door open with her foot.

"I volunteer at the veterinarian's office three days a week," Emily replied with a bright smile. "Dr. Winters lets me help with the animals. I really love it there." Her speech was filled with enthusiasm.

The bus driver remained in his seat, engine idling, watching over the scene. Fifteen minutes passed, then twenty. Judy found herself admiring his patience and quiet vigilance.

As the women carried in the last few packages, their conversation shifted. "Sometimes I'm worried about being all alone." Emily said.

"You're definitely not alone," Iris assured her, writing something on a small notepad she pulled from her pocket. "Here's my number. I'm just down the street at Alice's house every week cleaning."

Emily looked down at the paper, then back up at Iris with an expression of such genuine gratitude that Judy felt her own eyes grow misty.

"Thank you," Emily said simply.

"Pay it forward someday," Iris replied with a warm smile. "That's how it works."

As Iris turned to leave, she paused by the bus. To Judy's surprise, she knocked gently on the driver's window. The window hummed down, revealing a middle-aged man with kind eyes and salt-and-pepper hair.

"I just wanted to say thank you," Iris said. The driver looked confused. "For what, ma'am?"

"For waiting. For making sure she was okay. I saw you watching to make sure I wasn't some stranger causing trouble. We need more people looking out for each other like that."

The driver's face softened with understanding. "Part of the job, but not really in my job description, if you know what I mean."

"Those parts that aren't in the job description—they're often the most important," Iris replied.

Judy watched as Iris returned to her car, the bus finally pulling away from the curb. Emily stood on her porch for a moment, watching them leave before going back inside.

Something about the whole scene stirred Judy deeply. In twenty-five minutes, she had witnessed threads of community being woven together—the conscientious driver, the generous neighbor, the resilient young caregiver—each playing their part in a tapestry of human kindness.

Judy continued her walk, but her mind kept returning to Emily's white house. By the time she arrived home, she had made a decision. Tomorrow, she would bake her famous banana bread and take a different route—one that would lead her past the white house with blue trim. Perhaps Emily and her mother might enjoy a homemade treat. Perhaps they might need a retired teacher with plenty of free time and a lifetime of experience caring for others.

As Judy unlocked her front door, she smiled to herself. Her daily walk had always been about maintaining her physical health, but today it had nourished her spirit in unexpected ways. She had been reminded that sometimes the most important journeys aren't the ones that follow familiar paths, but those that lead us to unexpected moments of connection.

Sometimes, the best days begin with a detour.

"In a world where you can be anything, be kind. For it is kindness that turns moments into memories, strangers into friends, and simple days into extraordinary ones. The greatest gift we can offer is not found in packages, but in presence—in the willingness to see one another and to say with our actions: you are not alone." — Anonymous

This is a true story inspired by my sister Iris, who actually was the woman who pulled over to carry packages.

Three Simple Ways to Create a Good Day:

1. **Offer a Helping Hand**: Look for moments when someone is struggling—with groceries, directions, or even emotional weight. A simple "Can I help?" can transform their entire day.

2. **Practice the Five-Minute Pause**: Set aside five minutes in your day to stop and notice those around you. Who might need assistance? Sometimes awareness is the first step to connection.

3. **Carry Kindness Cards**: Write simple notes of encouragement or thanks to leave for service workers, neighbors, or strangers. A handwritten "You made a difference today" can create ripples of goodness far beyond what you'll ever see.

Pause long enough to hear the wisdom in silence— often the universe speaks most clearly when we're still.

10

The boy & the bear

✱ written by Adam Thomas

It was early May in Pennsylvania, the buds were just starting to bloom in the trees revealing delicate leaves of the most brilliant green. A green so light and bright, almost chartreuse which in some ways seemed unnatural but was most certainly beautiful.

Adam was riding his four wheeler up the winding country road which cut through the woods carved in the mountain with a sharp drop off on one side. It had likely started as a logging road many years before. He was heading home from his Grandpa's farm, a treat for him since he was just 13 and only recently allowed to make the trip alone. As he was pulling into his driveway, his neighbor Peg waved him down and told him that she had just seen a huge bear cross the road only a minute before he arrived. Adam had never seen a real live bear in the wild so without hesitation or caution, he took off in a dash into the woods.

He was able to move quickly as the woods were large and open. The forest floor was matted brown with last years leaves and the only plants popping up were a few ferns and patches of skunk cabbage. Adam continued to race, jumping over rocks and ducking under low hanging grape vines. Just as he reached an open trail he heard a loud crack that sounded like a tree falling and a huge roar that stopped him dead in his tracks. As he looked up the hill to his left he spotted the bear but his attention was quickly diverted to something else, something soft, something pure, something peaceful.

Two very young fawns hurried down the trail towards him. The spotted fawns came right next to him on each side and snuggled in against him looking for safety. For the next several minutes Adam knelt down at eye level and petted and rubbed the baby deer as he would a new puppy. The deer nuzzled his face and licked his ear. Lost in his bliss Adam had forgotten about the bear until he heard another crack on the trail up ahead.

He looked up quickly fearing the bear had moved in but was shocked to see the mother deer. She was pure white with a pink nose and the inside of her ears were a stunning fuzzy pink. He had never seen an albino deer before and it almost took his breath away. She was in a patch of dark green ferns and the contrast of white & green was so stark, she was spectacular. She stood with caution as she let out a soft but pointed snort. The two babies trotted away with their mother, looking back only once as if to say thank you.

Adam sat on a rock near the trail for a quite some time trying to absorb the joy and splendor that he had just witnessed. He never forgot how he felt that day and even at age 13 he knew it was God's glory and majesty shining down on him, something profound, something spiritual. He always remembered that he went into the woods to find something but instead something found him and it touched his life forever.

"Sometimes the greatest discoveries happen when we stop looking for what we think we want and open our eyes to what the world is trying to show us."

This story was written and inspired by my cousin Adam Thomas. It is based on his true story.

Three Things to Make You Have a Good Day:

1. The most beautiful moments in life are often unplanned and unexpected. What has happened lately, that was unplanned?

2. Nature speaks to those who take the time to listen. Take 5 minutes and sit somewhere outside.

3. Sometimes what you're seeking isn't nearly as wonderful as what's seeking you. Look for the unexpected around you.

Memories are the only treasures that grow more valuable when shared with others.

Kindness leaves no visible monument, yet somehow outlasts everything else we build

11

On a warm dusty highway

The Road to Puerto Peñasco

Anita watched the American SUVs zoom past, their drivers avoiding eye contact as they sped by on the desolate highway. Her convertible sat helplessly on the shoulder, the flat tire a mocking reminder that her new life in Mexico was beginning with a challenge she wasn't prepared for.

She wiped sweat from her brow and surveyed the mess surrounding her car. The contents of her trunk—her entire life packed into suitcases and boxes—now lay scattered by the roadside. Light items tumbled across the desert scrub, carried by the persistent wind that seemed determined to scatter her possessions across Sonora.

"This wasn't how it was supposed to begin," she muttered, trying to keep the panic from her voice.

Four hours earlier, she had left Phoenix with a heart full of dreams. Puerto Peñasco—her new home—represented everything she had yearned for: independence, adventure, sunsets over the Sea of Cortez, and a chance to reinvent herself away from the safety nets she'd always relied on.

Anita's mother had warned her. "Who's going to help you down there if something goes wrong?" she'd asked, concern around her eyes.

"I'll figure it out, Mom," she had answered confidently. "That's the whole point."

Now, standing alone on the highway with no cell service and the sun beating down, those words felt hollow. She had never changed a tire before—had never needed to. There had always been someone: a boyfriend, her father, AAA. The irony wasn't lost on her.

She had managed to put up the convertible top and was attempting to decipher the car manual when she heard music approaching—a cheerful ranchera melody floating on the hot desert air. The vehicle that pulled over was weathered, its once-blue paint faded to a patchy turquoise. It didn't inspire confidence, but the smile of the man who emerged did.

He gestured toward her tire with a questioning look, his eyebrows raised. Anita understood immediately.

"Mi español no es muy bueno," Anita replied, exhausting most of her Spanish vocabulary in one breath.

He nodded, smiled warmly, and pointed to himself, then to the tire, making a turning motion with his hands to indicate changing it.

A woman peered from the passenger window, offering a warm smile. In the back seat, two little girls with matching braids giggled and waved.

The man tapped his chest. "Francisco," he said simply, then gestured to his family with pride in his eyes.

The woman stepped out and, with a gentle smile and nod, immediately began helping Anita organize her scattered belongings. No words were needed to communicate her willingness to help. The little girls scrambled out, curious and eager to be part of the adventure.

"I'm sorry," Anita said, embarrassment washing over her. "I don't even have water to offer you."

The woman—Francisco's wife—waved away her concern with a gentle hand and a shake of her head. Her eyes conveyed everything: No need to worry. We help because you need help.

Francisco was already on his knees examining the tire. Anita tried to lay a blanket down for him to protect his clothes from the dusty road, but he politely refused with a gentle wave of his hand, seemingly unconcerned about the dirt.

As Francisco worked, the girls danced around the cars, singing along with the radio still playing from their open windows. Nobody complained about the heat or the interruption to their Sunday drive. There was no impatience, no checking of watches—just the unhurried rhythm of people connecting through a simple act of kindness.

When the tire was changed, Anita reached for her wallet. "Please," she said, extending two twenty-dollar bills and gesturing to Francisco.

Francisco shook his head firmly, hands up in a clear refusal.

Anita hesitated, then reached into her bag and pulled out two protein bars. She pantomimed eating, then pointed to the girls with a questioning look. When Francisco nodded, she handed each girl a protein bar, which they accepted with wide eyes and excited smiles as if she'd given them treasure.

Before they parted, Francisco insisted on making sure her car started properly. With thumbs up and universal gestures that needed no translation, he confirmed everything was working. The family watched her pull away, all of them waving as if sending off a friend rather than a stranger they'd met an hour ago.

In her rearview mirror, Anita saw the faded blue car grow smaller, but the impression the family left remained large in her heart. As she drove toward her new life, she reflected on how many American cars had passed her by—people who looked like her, spoke her language, but hadn't stopped.

It was her first lesson in her new country, delivered on a dusty highway: kindness transcends language, culture, and convenience. It asks nothing in return except perhaps that you pass it on.

Twenty years later, Anita still tells this story. Her Spanish is much better now, though far from perfect. She owns property in Puerto Peñasco, works remotely, and writes a column for the local paper. When tourists come to town and talk about the laid-back Mexican lifestyle—often with a hint of misunderstanding about "mañana" not meaning tomorrow—she smiles and sometimes shares her highway story.

"The mañana attitude isn't about procrastination," she writes in her column. "It's about understanding what deserves priority right now. Sometimes, helping a stranger is more important than keeping to your schedule."

And occasionally, when she sees a tourist stranded or struggling, she stops and gestures with a smile, asking with her eyes if they need help. Then she watches their face, wondering if they recognize the gift being offered—not just the help itself, but the invitation to see the world differently.

Would you stop? If you saw a stranger on an empty road, would you recognize that moment as an opportunity rather than an inconvenience? Anita did, but only after someone stopped for her first.

This story was inspired by my own experience during my first journey to Puerto Peñasco, Mexico. The events unfolded almost exactly as written. Sometimes I find myself scanning the faces in town, hoping to recognize that family who helped me when no one else would. I never got their names beyond "Francisco," never learned where they lived, never had the chance to truly thank them. But their kindness became the foundation to begin my new life here.

I only wish I could find them again—to tell them how that single act of compassion from strangers shaped my understanding of what it means to be part of a community. To let them know that twenty years later, a flat tire on a desert highway remains one of my most treasured memories.

Perhaps they'll never know the impact they had. But I honor them every time I stop for someone in need, every time I choose kindness over convenience. In this way, their gift continues, paying it forward through time.

> "In a world where you can be anything, be kind. For it is in giving that we receive, in pardoning that we are pardoned, and in kindness shown to strangers that we recognize our shared humanity." — Anonymous

Inspired by a true life event by the author.

Three Things to Brighten Your Day:

1. Look for opportunities to help rather than inconveniences to avoid. The most meaningful moments often come disguised as interruptions.

2. Remember that kindness requires no common language. A smile, a gesture, and willingness to help communicate more than words ever could.

3. When you feel stranded, trust that someone will stop. And when you see someone stranded, be that someone who stops.

The stranger who showed you kindness may never know they rearranged your entire universe that day.

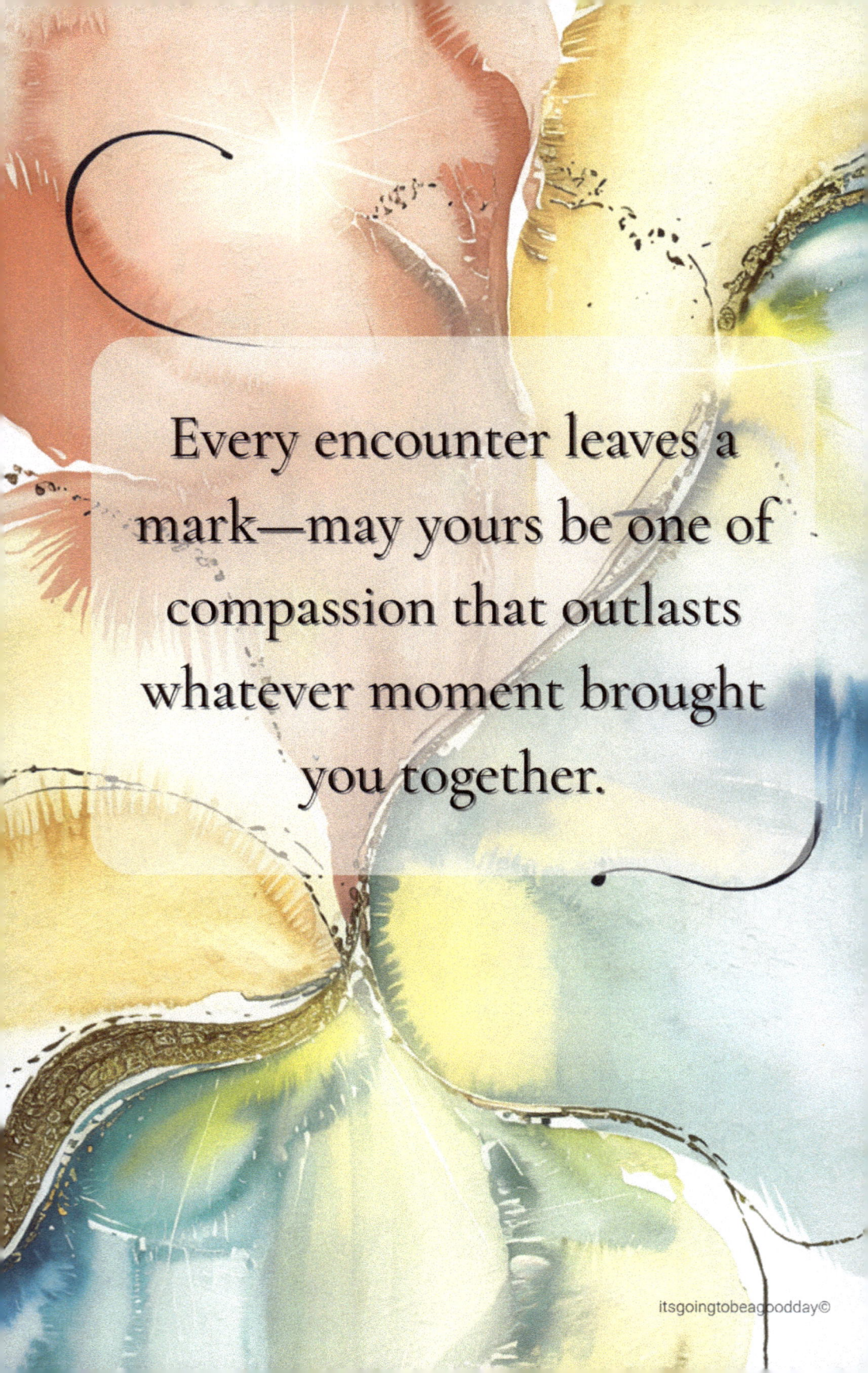

Every encounter leaves a mark—may yours be one of compassion that outlasts whatever moment brought you together.

12

The weight of memories

Michael stood in his father's garage, hands on his hips, surveying the mountains of boxes and bags that surrounded him. The air was thick with dust, and sunlight filtered through the single window in thin, determined shafts. It had been three weeks since Vernon moved to Pine Grove Assisted Living, and Michael had made little progress in clearing out the house.

"How did one man collect so much?" he muttered, lifting the flap of a cardboard box to find it filled with old fishing lures, none of which appeared to have ever touched water. His father had told him, "I don't want anything. Give it all away. Throw everything out."

His father had always been a collector—or a hoarder, depending on who you asked. Vernon Winters never met an object he couldn't imagine a future use for. His CB handle was "Bargain Hunter Extraordinaire". Ceramic figurines, National Geographic magazines dating back to the 1960s, pens, paint cans with just enough for "touch-ups," and more yardsticks than any handyman could use in three lifetimes.

Michael had been making piles: keep, donate, trash. The trash pile dwarfed the others.

In the corner of the garage, behind a broken television, Michael discovered the first garbage bag full of keychains. He untied it and poured the contents onto the concrete floor. Hundreds of keychains clattered out—advertisements for local businesses long shuttered, colorful plastic shapes, metal souvenirs from places his father had never visited.

"What in the world?" Michael whispered.

Over the next two days, he found nineteen more bags. Each one filled with keychains and fobs—thousands of them. Insurance companies, car dealerships, hardware stores, tourist traps, and banks. Some were still in their original packaging, others worn with age. The collection was both impressive and incomprehensible.

Michael stared at the mountain of keychains he had accumulated in the center of the garage. What possible purpose could his father have had for them? Where had they even come from? He couldn't imagine his father—a retired postal worker who rarely traveled—actively collecting these items.

With a sigh, Michael began shoveling them into fresh garbage bags. The recycling center would have to sort them out.

***

The next day, Michael visited his father at Pine Grove. Vernon sat in the common room, a plaid blanket across his lap despite the warmth of the day. His eyes brightened when he saw his son.

"Mikey! Come sit with me." He patted the chair beside him.

Michael settled in, relieved that today was a good day. The Alzheimer's had progressed quickly over the past year, and some days his father didn't recognize him at all.

"How's the house coming along?" Vernon asked.

"It's slow going, Dad. You've got a lot of stuff."

Vernon chuckled. "Your mother always said I never met a thing I didn't want to keep."

They talked about the weather, about the food at Pine Grove (terrible), and about Michael's job. As Michael stood to leave, Vernon suddenly gripped his arm with surprising strength.

"Did you find my keychains?" he asked, his eyes suddenly sharp with focus.

Michael's stomach dropped. "The keychains? You mean those advertising fobs?"

"Yes, yes. I must have thousands." Pride swelled in Vernon's voice. "What did you do with them?"

Michael swallowed hard. "I... I put them in bags for recycling," he admitted.

The light in Vernon's eyes dimmed. "Oh." Just that single syllable, but it carried the weight of profound disappointment.

"I'm sorry, Dad. I didn't realize they were important."

"Important?" Vernon's voice quavered. "I've been collecting them since before you were born."

Michael drove home with his father's disappointment heavy in his chest. He pulled into his driveway and stared at his garage, where twenty bags of keychains sat waiting for disposal. With a groan, he got out of the car.

It took him four hours to retrieve all the bags from various piles and consolidate the keychains into three large containers. The next morning, he lugged them to his car and drove back to Pine Grove.

***

"I brought something for you," Michael said, wheeling in a cart with the containers.

Vernon looked up from his jigsaw puzzle, confusion flickering across his face before recognition set in. "My keychains?"

Michael nodded. "All of them. I'm sorry I almost threw them away."

Vernon's weathered hands trembled as he opened the first container. He reached in and pulled out a handful, letting them run through his fingers like metallic rain. His face lit up with a joy Michael hadn't seen in years.

"I was afraid they were gone forever," Vernon said softly.

Michael sat beside his father. "Why did you collect them, Dad? There must be thousands here."

Vernon selected a faded keychain advertising "Pete's Auto Shop—Est. 1972." He rubbed his thumb over the worn lettering.

"Your mother and I used to go on Sunday drives. Every little town we passed through, every shop we visited, if they had a free keychain, I took one. After she died, I kept collecting them. Reminded me of those drives." He looked up at Michael. "Forty-five years of memories in these bins."

Michael's throat tightened. He'd nearly thrown away his parents' love story.

Vernon sifted through the keychains for a while longer, occasionally sharing a memory connected to one. Finally, he closed the lid on the container and pushed it toward Michael.

"I want you to have them."

Michael stared at his father. "But Dad, they're your collection."

Vernon shook his head. "What am I going to do with them in here? Besides," he said with a gentle smile, "now you know what they mean. Maybe you'll add a few of your own."

Later, as Michael loaded the containers back into his car, he realized that what he'd seen as worthless junk was actually the physical manifestation of his parents' joy—each keychain a moment, a memory, a tiny piece of a life well-lived.

He kept one out—a dolphin-shaped fob his mother must have picked up on their trip to Florida when Michael was ten—and attached it to his keys. The rest would go in his attic, not to gather dust, but to wait until he had time to sort through them properly, to learn the story of his parents' love, one keychain at a time.

"It's not what you look at that matters, it's what you see."— Henry David Thoreau

This story was told to me by my brother-in-law Mike Rafferty, his father and his thousands of keychains that Mike thew away and later retrieved, only to receive it back. He still has the keychains today.

Three Things to Have a Good Day

1. **Recognize that value isn't always visible to others**—what may seem like clutter to you might be someone else's treasure trove of memories.

2. **Take time to ask about the stories behind the things people hold dear**—you may discover depths of meaning you never imagined.

3. **Remember that the most precious collections aren't the items themselves**, but the moments and memories they represent.

True strength whispers
rather than shouts—it's
found in the quiet decision
to begin again, day after day.

In the quiet spaces between heartbeats, we find the courage to begin again— listen closely.

13
Coming through

The August heat pressed down on Jill's shoulders as she sat in her car, parked outside the medical building where Drs. Hartman, Reynolds, and Chen practiced. Her fingers gripped the steering wheel so tightly that her knuckles had gone white. She'd been sitting there for twenty minutes, unable to move, tears streaming down her face.

This wasn't how it was supposed to be. Her children—her heart beating outside her body—were being kept from her the entire summer. And now their father was refusing to communicate if and when he was sending her son back for the start of football camp, something her oldest son had been looking forward to for months.

She wiped her eyes with the back of her hand, smudging her carefully applied makeup. It didn't matter anymore. Nothing did, except getting her children back.

"Pull yourself together," she whispered to her reflection in the rearview mirror. Steel yourself. Be strong. Show them you're in control.

But she wasn't in control. She hadn't been since that terrible day when divorce and anger entered her life. The dissolving of a marriage something Jill never imagined for herself or her children.

With a deep breath, Jill opened her car door and stepped into the blistering heat. The medical building loomed before her, all glass and concrete, reflecting the unrelenting sun. She straightened her blouse, squared her shoulders, and began the long walk across the parking lot.

That's when she heard it.

The delicate notes of a piano drifted through the air from somewhere in the atrium of the building. Jill knew there was a baby grand piano in the large waiting area—she'd seen it on previous visits. But as she neared the entrance, the melody being played became unmistakable.

Her steps faltered, then stopped completely.

"In the Garden." Her grandmother Ferne's favorite hymn.

A sudden chill spread across Jill's skin despite the heat. Growing up as the middle child between a straight-A, homecoming queen older sister and an adorable baby sister, Jill had always felt invisible—except to Grandma Ferne. In her grandmother's eyes, Jill had always been special. Every summer spent at Ferne's farmhouse, the old upright piano in the living room would ring with that hymn as Ferne's weathered fingers danced across the yellowed keys. She played the harmonica too and loved to sing. Her voice would fill the house with everything from folk songs and hymns to nursery rhymes, but "In the Garden" was always her favorite.

It was the song they'd played at Ferne's funeral three years ago.

Jill stood frozen on the walkway, the melody washing over her. It couldn't be coincidence. Not this song, not now when she needed strength the most.

"Grandma?" she whispered.

No one was in the garden. The sound seemed to be coming from everywhere and nowhere at once.

A strange calm settled over Jill. She closed her eyes, letting the familiar melody surround her. In that moment, she could almost smell her grandmother's lavender hand cream, could almost feel the gentle squeeze of her hand.

Everything will be okay.

The words weren't spoken, not really, but Jill heard them all the same.

When she opened her eyes again, she walked into the building and saw an elderly woman seated at the baby grand piano in the atrium, her fingers gracefully moving across the keys as she played "In the Garden." Their eyes met briefly, and the woman smiled gently before finishing the piece. But even after the music stopped, the peace remained. Jill straightened her shoulders and walked toward the elevators with newfound resolve.

***

It wasn't the last time Grandma Ferne came through.

Three weeks later, after a particularly grueling day of single motherhood—the kids back but struggling with their new reality—Jill had escaped to the backyard patio with her old iPod. She needed just fifteen minutes of solitude, fifteen minutes to rebuild her strength.

She slipped in her earbuds, hit shuffle, and closed her eyes.

The first notes of "In the Garden" filled her ears.

Jill's eyes flew open. She looked down at the iPod screen in disbelief. She had never downloaded that hymn. It wasn't part of her carefully curated playlists of dance music and 90s alt-rock that helped her power through her daily runs.

Yet there it was, playing as clearly as if Grandma Ferne herself were sitting beside her.

Later that night, after the children were in bed, Jill searched through every playlist, every purchased song on her iPod. "In the Garden" was nowhere to be found.

***

"Do you think I'm crazy?" Jill asked her friend Beth over coffee the following week.

Beth considered the question carefully. "I don't think you're crazy. I think there are ways the people we love find to comfort us, even after they're gone."

"But a song appearing on my iPod and then disappearing?"

"When Max died," Beth said quietly, referring to her high school boyfriend who had been killed in a car accident their senior year, "the day after, on his birthday, I opened my daily devotional book. The passage was about how those we love never truly leave us." She shrugged. "Coincidence? Maybe. But it brought me comfort when I needed it most."

Jill nodded slowly. "Mike—the man I've been seeing—was having a really hard time yesterday. It was the first anniversary of his father's passing. He was sitting in his truck when 'Fortunate Son' started playing. It was his dad's favorite song. He said it wasn't the first time it's happened either. In times of need, he always seems to hear CCR playing somewhere."

"Random song or a message?" Beth smiled. "Does it matter if it brings peace?"

That night, as Jill tucked her youngest into bed, the little girl looked up at her with solemn eyes. "Mommy, does Grandma Ferne watch over us?"

The question caught Jill off guard. Her daughter had been only three when Ferne passed—barely old enough to remember her.

"Why do you ask, sweetie?"

"Because sometimes when you're sad, I hear humming. It sounds like the song in the music box Grandma gave me."

Jill's heart skipped a beat. She'd never told her children about hearing "In the Garden" or feeling her grandmother's presence.

"What do you think?" Jill asked carefully.

Her daughter smiled, already drifting toward sleep. "I think she helps you have good days when you're sad."

Jill leaned down and pressed a kiss to her daughter's forehead.

"I think you're right," she whispered. "You just have to listen."

"All I have seen teaches me to trust the Creator for all I have not seen." Ralph Waldo Emerson

Inspired by my very dear friend Jill Dumin, (you know what you mean to me). Her grandmother Ferne's favorite song was "In the Garden." Jill has no doubt that her grandmother came through when she needed her most. Sometimes our loved ones can help us have a good day. You just have to open your eyes, open your heart, and listen.

Three Suggestions to Have a Good Day:

1. **Notice the small moments of beauty** - Take five minutes to observe something in nature: the way light filters through leaves, birds singing their morning song, or how flowers turn toward the sun. These moments remind us that beauty persists even during difficult times.

2. **Listen for meaningful music** - Pay attention to songs that come on the radio, play unexpectedly, or get stuck in your head. Sometimes the universe speaks through melodies, and the right song at the right moment can shift your entire perspective.

3. **Share a memory with someone** - Call, text, or write to someone

about a happy memory you share. When we connect with others through shared experiences, we create ripples of joy that extend beyond ourselves.

Ferne

What if today's difficulties are simply tomorrow's wisdom, wearing a disguise?

itsgoingtobeagoodday©

14

Just keep bailing

At thirteen, Darrell thought he knew what it meant to be scared. He'd faced down bullies, survived his first school dance, and even managed to give a speech in front of his entire class. But he'd never known real fear until he saw that first splash of water seeping through the hull of their 21-foot soft top boat, somewhere between Prince Rupert and Glacier Bay, with nothing but the vast Alaskan wilderness surrounding them.

The morning had started with a sight that took his breath away - massive walls of ancient ice rising from the sea like nature's skyscrapers, their blue-white faces reflecting the early light. Chunks of ice dotted the steel-gray waters like diamonds scattered across dark velvet. Seals lounged on floating bergs, their sleek bodies gleaming in the bright northern sun, while bald eagles soared overhead, their wingspans casting shadows on the glacier faces.

"Dad?" His voice cracked, higher than usual as he spotted the leak. The summer adventure that was supposed to turn him into a man suddenly felt like it might do the opposite.

His father, James, looked up from where he was studying the water's intrusion. The late afternoon sun caught the silver in his hair, and Darrell couldn't help but notice how calm he seemed. Then again, this was a man who'd survived World War II, including the Battle of the Bulge, and who'd faced down threats far worse than a leaking boat in the Inside Passage of Alaska.

"Just keep bailing, son," James said simply, handing Darrell a bucket.

And so they bailed. Hour after hour, through waves that seemed determined to fill their small vessel faster than they could empty it. Their companion boat, carrying family friends from back home in Arizona, stayed close by, ready to help if needed. But James seemed certain they could handle it themselves.

The Inside Passage revealed its majesty even in their moment of crisis. Towering spruce and hemlock trees lined the shoreline like silent statues, their reflection perfect in the protected waters of hidden coves. Waterfalls cascaded down cliff faces, their spray creating rainbows in the slanting light. In the distance, snow-capped peaks pierced the clouds, and occasionally they'd spot a brown bear strolling along the shoreline, fishing for salmon in the pristine waters.

"You know what your grandfather used to tell me?" James asked as they worked, their movements falling into a rhythm with the waves. "He said life's going to throw water at you. Sometimes it's a sprinkle, sometimes it's a storm. The trick isn't avoiding the water - it's learning how to bail."

Darrell's arms ached, but he kept going. Somehow, his father's matter-of-fact approach made the situation feel less dire. They weren't fighting for survival; they were just solving a problem, one bucket at a time, surrounded by some of the most breathtaking scenery on Planet Earth.

As the sun began to set, painting the Alaskan sky in brilliant oranges and pinks that reflected off the glacier faces like nature's light show, Darrell realized something had changed. The fear was still there, but it had transformed into something else - a kind of quiet determination. The vastness of Alaska had a way of putting things in perspective. Against the backdrop of thousand-year-old ice and mountains that touched the clouds, their leak seemed manageable, just another challenge to overcome.

Some lessons couldn't be taught in the safety of dry land.

His daughter settled into the chair beside him. "Is that why you always say 'just keep bailing' when things get tough?"

Darrell laughed, remembering the way the midnight sun had painted the water in impossible colors, how pods of orcas had surfaced alongside their small boat, their black fins cutting through water as smooth as glass. "Exactly. Whether it's a tough project at work, a challenging relationship, or even raising a teenager" - he winked at his daughter -"sometimes the only way through is to just keep bailing."

He opened the book to a particular photograph - a skinny twelve-year-old boy standing proudly on the bow of a small boat, glaciers looming behind him. "You know, your grandfather's war stories were legendary, but he never talked about them much. Instead, he taught me about courage through this trip. He showed me that bravery isn't about not being scared - it's about being scared and doing what needs to be done anyway."

The study fell quiet as they looked at the old photographs together. Outside, a summer storm was brewing, not unlike the ones Darrell had faced in Alaska all those years ago. But now, every rumble of thunder brought a smile to his face.

"Your great-grandfather wrote in this book that 'adventure isn't about conquering nature - it's about discovering what you're made of.' Turns out, sometimes you have to spring a leak to find out just how strong you can be."

His daughter looked thoughtful. "Do you think I'll ever have an adventure like that?"

Darrell closed the book gently. "Life has a way of providing adventures when we need them most. And when it does, just remember -whatever water comes your way, you can handle it. Just keep bailing, and before you know it, you'll find yourself with a story worth telling."

And as the storm outside grew stronger, Darrell began to share more details about that summer of 1972, when two small boats from Arizona dared to tackle the Inside Passage, and a thirteen-year-old boy learned that sometimes the simplest advice - "just keep bailing" - could carry you through the biggest challenges life had to offer.

"The journey of a thousand miles begins with a single step." - Lao Tzu (Ancient Chinese philosopher, traditionally 6th century BC)

*This short story was inspired by true events and a trip taken by four men, and two teenagers (my husband) who threw caution to the wind and thought anything was possible. Confronting huge oceans, ice flows, and gigantic glaciers with an adventurous spirit, they faced the trials and tribulations of taking a 21ft soft top boat and a 23ft power boat from Arizona to the inside passage of Alaska. With lady luck not always on their side they braved the 5 week adventure and made it a lifetime memory.

Their adventure story written almost 40 years is available in the book, "Inside the Inside Passage, Power Boating to Alaska" by Donald S Riggs.

"It will make you laugh and wonder, what in the world they were thinking. Through their eyes take a passenger seat on the journey "Inside the inside passage".

***

Three "It's Going to Be a Good Day" things to try today:

1. If you have a big problem try to think about it in smaller steps.

2. If you can write down one thing that could help the resolution.

3. Think about a time in your past when a big problem was resolved by starting small.

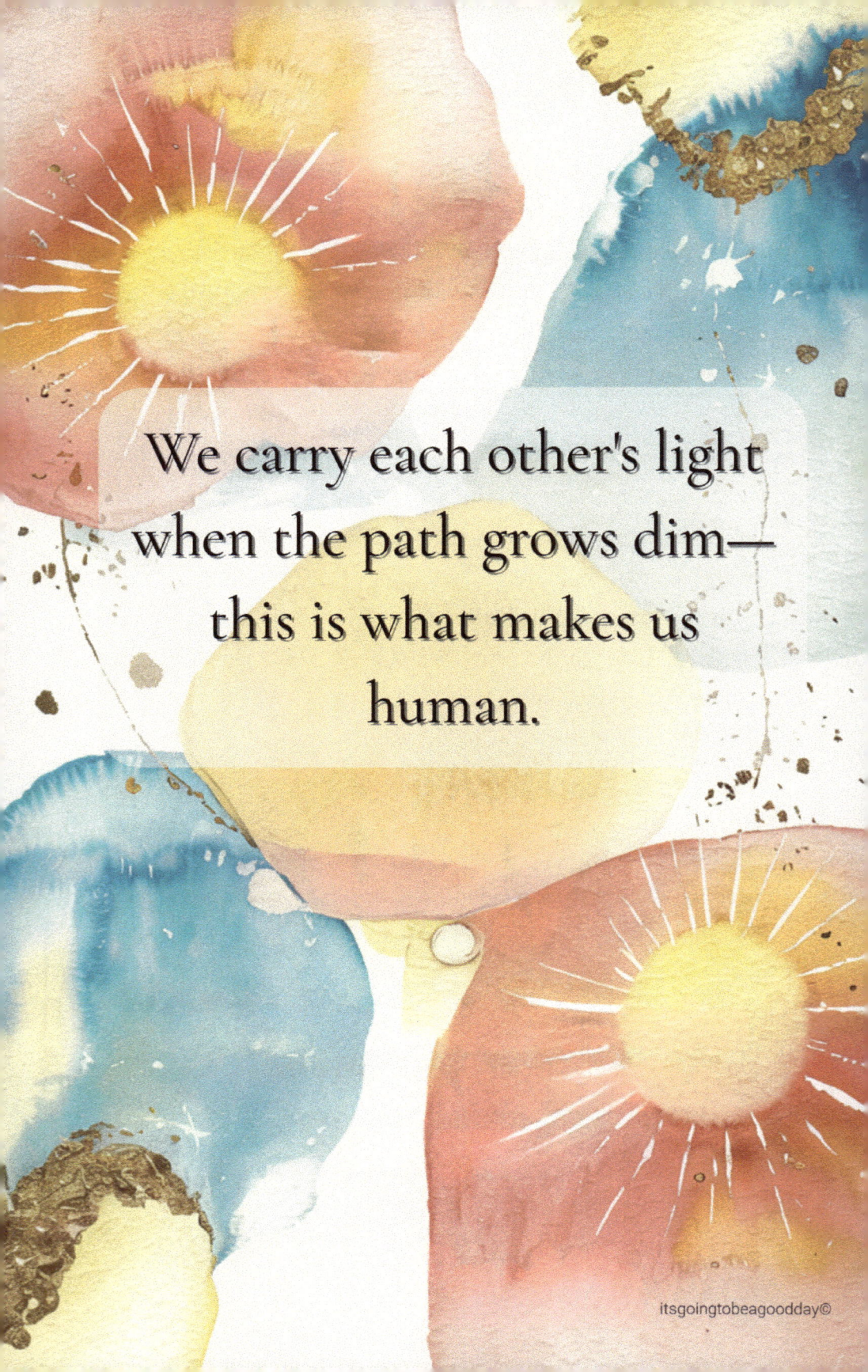

We carry each other's light
when the path grows dim—
this is what makes us
human.

oo loo loo

Perhaps true courage is simply kindness, practiced when it's hardest to offer.

15

Ice cream lessons

Chris exhaled slowly as she parked her minivan outside Miss Lynn's School of Music. Three-year-old Noah pressed his palms against the window, his eyes fixed on the Victorian house with its peeling yellow paint and grand piano visible through the bay window.

"Do I have to?" Noah whispered, his lower lip quivering.

"Yes, sweetie," Chris said, unbuckling him. "Piano lessons are good for you."

"But ice cream is better for me," he protested, eyeing one-and-a-half-year-old Ali and five-year-old nephew Elijah in the backseat, both grinning with anticipation.

Chris ruffled Noah's hair. "Piano first, then ice cream next week. I promise."

"Is he being punished?" Elijah asked innocently.

"No, honey, he's being cultured," Chris replied, though the distinction was probably lost on all three children.

She escorted Noah to the door, where Miss Lynn—a woman whose posture suggested she'd been born with a metronome for a spine—greeted them with a tight smile.

"We'll work on his finger placement today," Miss Lynn said, as if discussing a crucial surgical procedure.

Back in the minivan, Chris turned to her remaining passengers. "Who wants ice cream?"

The resulting cheer nearly blew out the windows.

Ten minutes later, they pulled into Silver Bell, the local ice cream tasty freeze that had been serving the town since Chris herself was a child. The summer heat had drawn a crowd, with a line snaking out the door.

"Chocolate!" Ali clapped her hands.

"Mint chocolate chip," Elijah corrected. "It's superior in every way."

Chris smiled at her nephew's vocabulary. He'd been staying with them for the summer while her sister traveled for work, and he'd clearly been spending time with his grandfather, who spoke as if always addressing a jury.

"Both flavors are great choices," Chris said diplomatically, gathering her purse. "Let's go."

The ice cream excursion was a sticky success. Ali ended up with more chocolate on her face than in her stomach, while Elijah meticulously consumed his mint chocolate chip one precise bite at a time. Chris savored her coffee-flavored scoop, mentally calculating how much time left until she had to pick up Noah from his lesson.

It wasn't until they returned to the minivan, three empty cones and multiple napkins later, that disaster struck.

Chris reached for her keys and found nothing. Her pockets were empty. Her purse yielded only the usual chaos of receipts, half-eaten granola bars, and toy cars—but no keys.

Peering through the driver's side window, she spotted them dangling from the ignition, mocking her from behind locked doors.

"Oh no," she groaned, resting her forehead against the glass.

A middle-aged man walking by noticed her distress. "Locked out, huh?"

Soon, a small crowd had gathered, each person offering increasingly unhelpful advice.

"Call 911," suggested an elderly woman clutching a poodle.

"No, don't waste their time," countered a teenager without looking up from his phone. "Call the dealership."

"YouTube it," offered another passerby. "There are tutorials for everything."

"I got this," Chris said, waving them off. "In the old days, we used to use a wire hanger."

As if on cue, the owner of Silver Bell emerged with a wire hanger. "Thought you might need this," he said with a knowing smile.

Chris accepted it gratefully. "My dad taught me this trick when I was sixteen."

She straightened the hanger, creating a hook at one end while explaining to her audience how this was done "back in the day." Ali clapped excitedly, while Elijah watched with scholarly interest.

"See, you slide it down between the window and the weather stripping," Chris narrated, performing the action. "Then you hook it around the lock mechanism and pull up."

Five minutes passed. Then ten. The hanger refused to catch on anything useful.

"Maybe try from the passenger side?" someone suggested.

Chris nodded, sweat beading on her forehead. She moved around the vehicle, determined to prove that analog solutions still worked in a digital world.

Her audience had grown, with some people placing informal bets on her success. Ali had started singing the alphabet song, currently on her third repetition, while Elijah silently observed his aunt's increasingly desperate attempts.

"Dad used to do this all the time," Chris muttered to herself. "How hard can it be?"

The sun beat down mercilessly. Fifteen minutes had passed. The wire hanger had bent into shapes that would make a sculptor proud. Chris's determination had morphed into grim stubbornness.

"I can do this," she insisted to no one in particular.

Elijah, who had been quietly contemplating the situation, finally spoke up. "Aunt Chris?"

"Not now, sweetie," Chris said, jiggling the wire with renewed vigor. "Almost got it."

"But Aunt Chris," he persisted, tugging at her shirt.

"Just a minute, Elijah," she said, convinced she felt something catch inside the door.

"Aunt Chris!" His voice rose slightly. "Why don't you reach in through the back window?"

Chris froze. Slowly, she turned toward the back of the minivan. There, partially rolled down about four inches, was the back passenger window—the one she'd opened to give Ali some air.

The crowd fell silent. Ali stopped singing. Even the poodle seemed to hold its breath.

Without a word, Chris walked to the back window, reached her arm through the opening, unlocked the back door, climbed in, and pressed the unlock button for all doors. The familiar chirp of the locks releasing sounded like a punchline to a joke everyone had been waiting too long to hear.

The crowd erupted in laughter and applause. Chris took a theatrical bow from inside the van.

"Sometimes," she announced to her audience, emerging from the driver's door, "it takes a five-year-old to show us the obvious."

Later, as they drove to pick up Noah from his piano lesson, Elijah asked, "Were you really going to get that door open with the hanger?"

Chris laughed. "Probably not. But you know what happens? We get so focused on doing things the way we've always done them that we miss the simpler solution right in front of us."

"Like when I try to build a tower with just the red blocks," Ali contributed surprisingly.

"Exactly," Chris nodded. "Sometimes God is practically pulling on our coat strings saying, 'Hey, look at the back window!' but we're too busy with our wire hangers."

"God wears a coat?" Ali asked, confused.

"It's a metaphor, Ali," Elijah explained solemnly ."A figure of speech that makes a comparison between two unrelated things."

Chris caught his eye in the rearview mirror and winked. "Sometimes the wisest person in the room is the one who sees what everyone else misses."

Elijah beamed.

When they arrived at Miss Lynn's, Noah emerged looking surprisingly cheerful.

"How was piano?" Chris asked, expecting complaints.

"Great!" He climbed into the van. "Miss Lynn let me play 'Chopsticks' instead of scales today!"

"See?" Chris said to no one in particular. "Sometimes the back window is open when you least expect it."

Noah looked confused. "What back window?"

"I'll tell you over ice cream next week," Chris promised. "It's quite a story."

"We are all in the gutter, but some of us are looking at the stars." — Oscar Wilde

Inspired by a true story told to me by my brother Pastor Peter Kaltenbaugh Jr.

It's Going to Be a Good Day
Three Ways to Look Through the Back Window Today:

1. Take a different route home and notice something new in your familiar surroundings.

2. Ask a child for their perspective on a problem you've been struggling with.

3. Before tackling a challenge, pause and ask yourself: "What obvious solution might I be overlooking?"

Between who you were and
who you are becoming lives
your most beautiful story

16

Grace beyond goodbye

Ginny sat frozen while Dr. Murphy waited for her to comprehend what he had just told her. Really comprehend it. Like Ginny, Ray's eyes grew wet. The room was silent, suspended in a moment that would alter the course of their lives forever.

Ginny was pregnant. Five months along.

"We can't be sure the baby is... unaffected... by the treatments, of course," Dr. Murphy stammered. "There is no sure way to tell what harm has been done thus far..."

Ginny felt panicked. This was not good news. Not this time. She fought to keep the lump in her throat from erupting into the air like a terrible, devastating volcano. How could she do this to Ray and the other children? Her chest began to heave as her body unsuccessfully put forth its best effort to sob. She was just too weak.

Her body couldn't create life and fight death at the same time, could it?

She immediately knew she would not abort her child. Not this far along. Regardless, it was simply not an option for her, even if it meant saving her own life. Still, Ginny recognized that continuing the pregnancy would be more than her ragged body could endure.

Ray went to her, gently placing his hands around her pale, gaunt face, holding her head for her. "My love, this is not the end," he whispered. "This is a new beginning."

***

That night, after the children were asleep, Ginny stood at the window of their farmhouse. The Iowa winter pressed coldly against the glass, but somewhere behind those clouds was a moon, stars, an entire universe spinning in perfect rhythm.

"I've made my decision," she said when Ray entered the room.

He nodded, already knowing. "The treatments."

"I'm stopping them. For the baby." Her voice was stronger than it had been in months.

Ray crossed the room and stood beside her. "Are you sure?"

Ginny took his hand and placed it on her slight bump. "This child is the piece of me that gets to stay. Even when I can't."

Ray's breath caught. "How can I raise four children without you?"

"The same way you do everything else," Ginny smiled faintly. "One day at a time. And every morning, you'll wake up and say what we always say..."

"It's going to be a good day," they finished together.

***

Spring came, and with it, a miracle. As Ginny grew weaker, the life inside her grew stronger. The baby kicked and tumbled as if trying to share some vital energy with her mother.

"I think she's dancing," Ginny told Susie one afternoon as they felt the movements together.

"She?" Ten-year-old Susie's eyes widened.

"Just a feeling," Ginny smiled. "Her name will be Carly. It means 'stren gth.'"

That night, while Ray thought she was sleeping, Ginny wrote letters. One for each birthday, graduation, wedding day. Moments she knew she would miss. The last letter she wrote began: For my granddaughter, Ginger...

Carly Elizabeth was born on a morning when sunlight streamed through the hospital windows like liquid gold. She had a tuft of blonde hair—just like her mother's had been before the treatments—and lungs that worked perfectly well, with bright blue eyes full of life, announcing her arrival to the world with robust cries.

Dr. Murphy called it a miracle. The baby was healthy, despite everything.

Ginny held her daughter against her chest, memorizing the weight of her, the scent of her head, the tiny fingers that curled instinctively around her own. "Remember," she whispered to Ray as she finally placed the baby in his arms. "Every morning..."

"It's going to be a good day," he promised, tears falling freely now. "I'll tell her every day."

Three weeks later, as summer bloomed across the farmland, Ginny slipped away while the children played in the yard and Carly slept peacefully in the crook of her arm. The last thing she saw was sunlight breaking through the bedroom curtains, painting the room in warm gold.

Carly grew up surrounded by stories of her mother—not sad ones, but stories of Ginny's laugh, her stubbornness, the way she danced in the kitchen while making breakfast. Every morning, without fail, Ray would wake his children with the same words: "It's going to be a good day."

Sometimes it wasn't. Sometimes it was terrible.

But they said it anyway.

***

When Carly's twelve-year-old daughter Ginger was diagnosed with juvenile diabetes, Carly felt the universe had played a cruel joke. Hadn't her family suffered enough? But that first night in the hospital, as Ginger finally slept, she found herself at the window watching the sunrise breakthrough storm clouds.

"It's going to be a good day," she whispered, and somehow, she believed it.

She raised Ginger with insulin shots and glucose monitors, with careful meal planning and midnight blood checks. But also with laughter, with dancing in the kitchen, with stories of the grandmother who had chosen life even when facing death. Ginger became an ambassador for juvenile diabetes and raised money all her life to fight the disease.

When Ginger was sixteen, she found the letter—yellowed with age, her name written in elegant script she didn't recognize.

Dearest Ginger,

We've never met, but I know you. You are strength. You are grace. You carry the best parts of all of us. When life feels unfair, remember that the greatest gifts often come from the deepest sacrifices. Your mother lives because I chose her. You live because your mother chooses you every day.

I don't know what challenges you'll face, but I know this: you come from a line of women who turn darkness into light.

It's going to be a good day, sweet girl.

With eternal love, Your grandmother, Ginny

***

Aspen Ginger Marshall stood in her laboratory at the Arizona State University Medical Center, adjusting her microscope. At thirty, she'd dedicated her career to oncology research, specifically breast cancer—the disease that had taken the great-grandmother she'd never met, and had plagued her grandmother.

"Dr. Marshall," her assistant called from the doorway, "the results are in."

Aspen's hands trembled slightly as she reviewed the data. The compound they'd developed—one they'd been testing for months—had shown unprecedented effectiveness in targeting triple-negative breast cancer cells while leaving healthy cells intact.

"This is it," she whispered. "This is what we've been looking for."

That evening, Aspen drove to the Lookout Mountain Park in the desert. The setting sun broke through the saguaros, casting long shadowy fingers across the desert floor.

"We did it, Great Grandma," she said softly. "Not a complete cure yet, but a beginning." She placed her hand on the locket she wore around her neck, in it three woman in her life that made her who she was her mother Ginger, her grandmother Carly and her great grandmother Ginny. "The journals are already calling it the Marshall-Thompson Protocol, but I've submitted the paperwork to rename it."

Aspen smiled through her tears. "From now on, it will be called the Ginny Protocol. Because of you, thousands of mothers will get to stay. Thousands of daughters will never have to wonder."

As she turned to leave, the last rays of sunlight warmed her face, and Aspen felt a certainty deeper than science, stronger than data.

Tomorrow was going to be a good day.

***

"The most beautiful people we have known are those who have known defeat, known suffering, known struggle, known loss, and have found their way out of the depths. These persons have an appreciation, a sensitivity, and an understanding of life that fills them with compassion, gentleness, and a deep loving concern. Beautiful people do not just happen." - Elisabeth Kübler-Ross

Inspired by the true life story of my friend Carla Engel, whose working manuscript shared the incredible details of her family's journey. Carla's mother Ginny found out she was pregnant with Carla five months into her breast cancer treatments. This story is inspired from Carla's own writing, and we encourage her to complete and publish her manuscript so the world can know Ginny's full story. Carla has two children, Ginger and Nick, and we are so blessed and grateful to have Carla as our friend in this world. While Nick and Ginger don't yet have children of their own, we hold hope for a little Aspen who might one day complete the circle—bringing healing and purpose to a journey that began with one mother's ultimate act of love.

Three Suggestions for Having a Good Day (Inspired by the Story):

1. **Begin with Intention:** Start each morning by saying aloud "It's

going to be a good day" – just as Ginny's family did. This simple act of setting a positive intention can shift your mindset even during difficult times.

2. **Find the Sunlight:** Look for moments of beauty and breakthrough in each day, like the sunlight breaking through clouds in the story. Even on the hardest days, these small moments of grace can sustain us.

3. **Create Ripples of Love:** Remember that our choices today – especially the sacrificial ones – can create positive ripples that extend far beyond our own lives, just as Ginny's choice ultimately led to healing for countless others.

***

"Do not judge each day by the harvest you reap but by the seeds that you plant." - Robert Louis Stevenson

The soul expands in proportion to how fully we allow ourselves to love what may never stay.

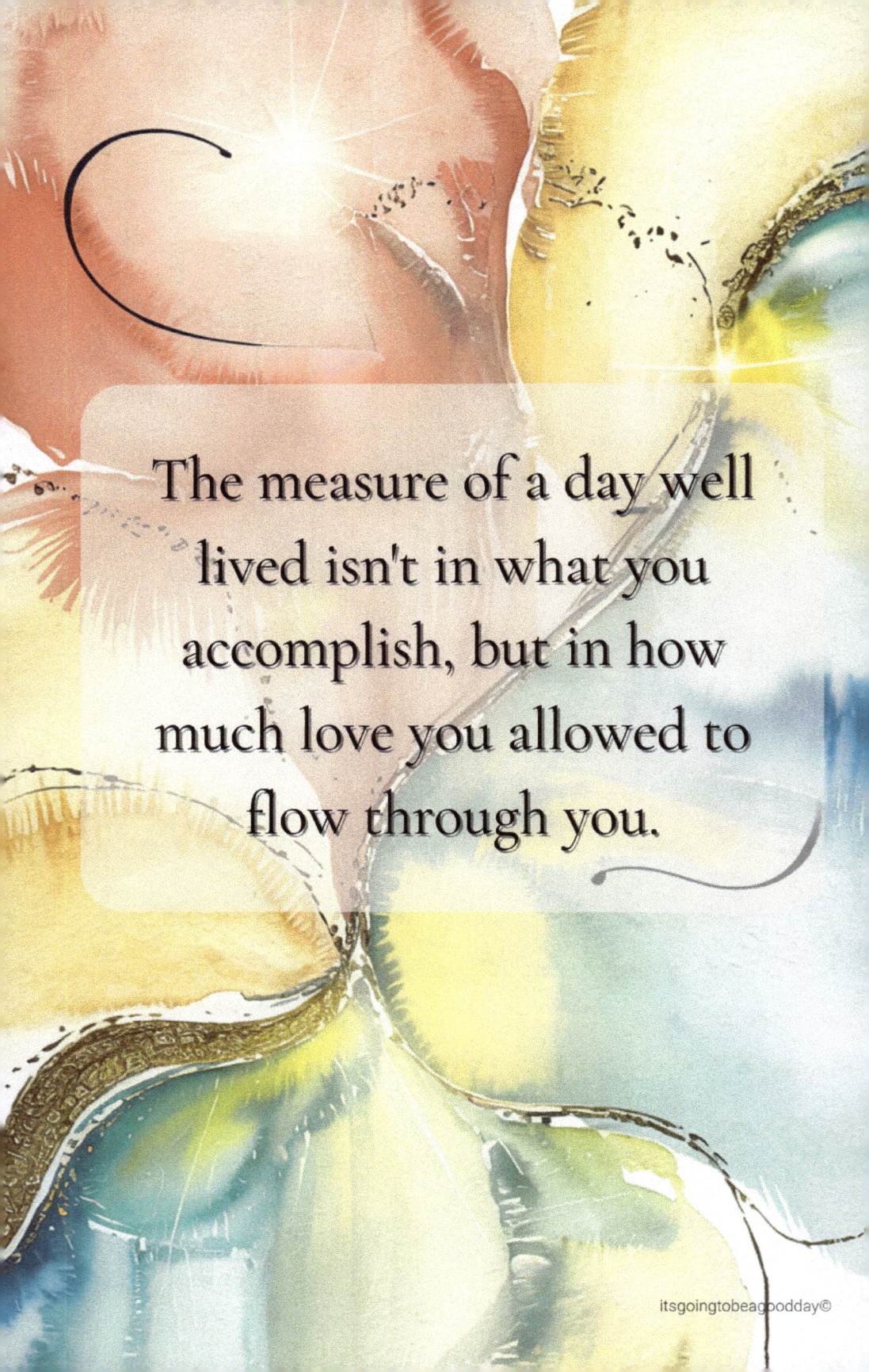

The measure of a day well lived isn't in what you accomplish, but in how much love you allowed to flow through you.

17
Throwing corn

The smell of autumn in western Pennsylvania is something you never forget. It's a unique blend of crisp air, fallen leaves, and wood smoke that seems to seep into your bones and stay there forever. It was on nights like these—when the maple and oak trees had turned their fiery colors and the evening air carried just the right chill—that we'd gather for what the neighborhood kids called "tic-tacking."

Though we didn't know it then, this tradition of throwing corn kernels dated back generations. Local newspapers like LebTown would later report that "tic-tacking" had been documented as far back as 1891 in The Galesburg Enterprise, with similar accounts appearing in Pennsylvania's New Castle Herald in 1912 and Latrobe Bulletin in 1969. It was most common in corn-growing regions like ours, a harmless ritual of mischief night—the evening before Halloween—when children were somehow permitted their annual taste of controlled rebellion.

But to us, it was just something passed down from one generation of bored rural kids to the next, a peculiar rite of passage in our little corner of Soap Hollow.

"You ready for tonight?" My best friend Jamie whispered during fifth-period science.

I nodded, feeling that familiar flutter of excitement and fear in my stomach. "Got the bags?"

"Three of 'em. My dad doesn't even ask anymore when I take corn from the feed bin."

That evening, six of us met at the edge of Old Man Miller's farm as darkness settled over the hollow. Miller wasn't really that old, probably only in his forties, but anyone over thirty qualified as ancient in our teenage estimation. He knew what we were up to—everyone did—but he turned a blind eye as Jamie and I filled our canvas sacks with dried feed corn from his silo.

"Just don't let me catch you," he'd say with a wink that told us he absolutely wanted us to get away with it.

By dusk, we were positioned perfectly—crouched above the steep embankment that overlooked the winding country road, hidden by the shadow of maple trees and the growing darkness. The spot was ideal: cars had to slow for the sharp curve, and the bank was steep enough that we could throw and retreat in seconds.

"Car coming!" hissed Sarah, the only girl brave enough to join our mischief.

We all fell silent, clutching handfuls of corn, hearts racing. The distant headlights grew brighter as they approached the curve. The timing had to be perfect—too soon and they'd see us, too late and we'd miss.

"Now!" Jamie whispered, and six hands released a barrage of corn kernels that rained down on the passing sedan with a sound like hail on a tin roof.

The brake lights flashed red, illuminating our faces for one terrifying second before the car accelerated again, continuing down the country road. We collapsed into silent laughter, high-fiving each other in the darkness.

"That's one!" Todd announced, keeping count as he always did.

We settled back into position, waiting for the next victim. Sometimes we'd wait for an hour between cars on this seldom-traveled road. Those were the best moments—just sitting there in the darkness, telling stories, feeling like we owned the night, like we were getting away with something extraordinary.

It was on our fourth car of the night that everything changed. The corn had barely left our hands when the car screeched to a halt, tires protesting against the pavement. The driver's door flung open.

"I got you now, you little punks!" The voice was unmistakable—Scott Lange, who'd graduated a few years before us and was known for his hot temper.

Panic hit like a physical blow. We scattered, abandoning our corn bags and scrambling up the embankment into the woods. I ran faster than I'd ever run in my life, branches whipping at my face, the sound of my own heartbeat drowning out everything else. Behind me, I could hear Jamie's labored breathing and the crashing sounds of the others fleeing through the underbrush.

"Please God," I prayed silently, "I'll never do this again if you just let us get away safe."

We ran until our lungs burned, finally collapsing behind the remnants of an old stone wall deep in the woods. Only then did we realize Scott wasn't actually chasing us. In the distance, we could hear his laughter echoing through the trees.

"He's just messing with us," Jamie gasped between breaths. "He probably did the same thing when he was our age."

Walking home that night, covered in scratches and burrs, I felt something shift inside me. Not regret exactly—we hadn't hurt anyone with our soft corn missiles—but a new awareness of how quickly harmless fun could turn to real fear, and how the line between mischief and meanness wasn't always clear.

Years later, when I returned to Soap Hollow after college, I drove down that same winding road one autumn evening. I slowed at the familiar curve, half-expecting to hear the patter of corn on my roof. But the embankment stood empty, the tradition apparently faded away like so many others.

I pulled over and climbed the bank, surprised at how much smaller it seemed than in my memories. Standing there in the gathering dusk, I could almost see us—young, fearless, believing we had discovered something uniquely ours in this simple act of rebellion.

My phone buzzed. A message from Jamie, now a father of two: "Remember tic-tacking? My son asked to borrow corn from the feed bin. Should I be worried?"

I smiled, typing back: "Tell him about the night Scott Lange stopped. Some lessons are better learned secondhand."

Because that's what tic-tacking taught me—not that having fun is wrong, but that understanding consequences is part of growing up. In today's world, such pranks would likely end with police reports and lawsuits rather than laughter. Yet I still treasure those memories, not for the mischief itself, but for what it represented: that brief, magical time when the night belonged to us, when fear and friendship mingled into something that felt like freedom.

The world changes. Childish things must be put away. But the ripple effect of traditions like tic-tacking continues, flowing through generations like an underground stream, occasionally bubbling to the surface in newspaper articles and reminiscences.

I later learned that what we did on those autumn nights was part of a tradition that stretched from Kansas to Pennsylvania, documented in yellowed newspaper clippings dating back to the 1890s. It was never meant to harm—just good clean fun, a chance to be a goblin for the night, to feel that delicious thrill of minor mischief in a world that increasingly leaves little room for such innocent transgressions.

Sometimes, driving down a country road on an autumn evening, I roll down my window and let that familiar smell of fallen leaves and woodsmoke fill my car. And for just a moment, I'm thirteen again, corn in hand, waiting for headlights to appear around the bend, believing this is what it means to be alive.

I wonder if somewhere in Soap Hollow tonight, a new generation of kids is crouched in those same woods, bags of corn at the ready, keeping alive a tradition that has weathered more than a century of changing times—a testament to the enduring human need to occasionally step outside the lines, even if just by the width of a corn kernel.

> "Youth is happy because it has the capacity to see beauty. Anyone who keeps the ability to see beauty never grows old." — Franz Kafka

If you ever went tic-tacking, cow-tipping or snipe-hunting this story is for you. Inspired by my neighborhood friends of Soap Hollow, Pennsylvania.

Three Ways to Have a Good Day

1. **Revisit a cherished memory.** Take time today to close your eyes and fully recall a joyful moment from your youth. Notice the details—the smells, sounds, and feelings that made it special.

Sharing this memory with someone else multiplies its power.

2. **Embrace harmless mischief.** Do something slightly unexpected today. Leave an anonymous note of encouragement for a neighbor, hide a small gift for a loved one to find, or take a different route on your daily walk. Small surprises keep the spirit young.

3. **Connect across generations.** Ask a young person about their childhood traditions or share one of yours. The bridge between generations is built on these shared stories of what it means to be young, no matter the era.

The space between who we are and who we might become is bridged by countless small acts of courage.

18

A different kind of solution

It was one of those Phoenix summer days when the temperature climbed past 120 degrees, the kind of heat that made the air shimmer and dance above the pavement. Inside their comfortable home, ten-year-old Tyler sat cross-legged on the couch, deeply absorbed in his video game, wearing a thick gray sweatshirt and sweatpants as if it were the middle of winter.

His mother Nadine paused in the doorway, shaking her head at the sight. "Tyler, honey, you must be roasting! Go upstairs and change into a t-shirt and shorts."

"Okay, Mom," Tyler mumbled, eyes never leaving the screen.

Twenty minutes later, Nadine returned to find Tyler still bundled up in his winter wear, his forehead glistening with sweat as his thumbs worked the game controller.

"Tyler, I thought I told you to change. You're going to overheat in those clothes!"

"I know, Mom. I'll do it," he replied, reaching a save point in his game.

Another fifteen minutes passed, and Nadine's patience was wearing thin. She stood in front of the TV, hands on her hips. "Young man, this is the third time I'm telling you - you need to cool yourself down. Go put on a t-shirt and shorts right now!"

Tyler finally looked up, his face bright with conviction. "But Mom, I did take care of it!" He pulled at his sleeve, and water dripped onto the couch.

"See? I went to the bathroom and soaked all my clothes in cold water. Now I'm nice and cool!"

Nadine stood there, momentarily speechless, caught between exasperation and amazement at her son's unusual solution. She wanted to scold him for getting the couch wet, wanted to explain why this wasn't the best approach - but then she saw his proud smile, the genuine belief that he'd solved the problem, and she couldn't help but laugh.

Later that evening, after Tyler had finally changed into weather-appropriate clothing, Nadine called her sister to share the story. "You know what struck me?" she said, still chuckling. "In his own way, he did solve the problem. It wasn't the solution I would have chosen - not by a long shot - but he found a way that made sense to him."

Her sister laughed. "Sounds like that time Dad fixed the leaky roof with duct tape and a plastic tablecloth. Not exactly conventional, but it got us through that storm!"

"Exactly!" Nadine replied. "It reminds me of something Mom used to say: 'There are a hundred ways to get from here to there. Some are straight lines, some are scenic routes, and some might get you a little wet along the way.'"

Looking back, Nadine realized that day taught her something important about parenting - and about life. Sometimes the solutions our children find might seem strange or imperfect to us, but they're learning to think creatively, to solve problems in their own way. And isn't that what we want for them? The confidence to think independently, even if their solutions occasionally leave puddles on the couch?

After all, life rarely presents us with perfect solutions. Sometimes the best answer isn't the most obvious one, and sometimes the path we choose might raise a few eyebrows. But as long as we're willing to think creatively and take responsibility for our choices - even if that means sitting in wet sweatpants on a hot summer day - we're growing, learning, and finding our own way through the world.

And sometimes, that's exactly the solution we need.

***

"It is common sense to take a method and try it. If it fails, admit it frankly and try another. But above all, try something." - Franklin D. Roosevelt (1882-1945)

* Inspired by my walking buddy Nadine who walks 4-5 miles a day— with me by the sea. A true story of her son when he was younger.

***

It's Your Good Day.

Make it count. Make it joyful. Make it yours.

Three Steps to a Good Day:

1. Ask a friend or family member how they would solve a small problem you've been facing; their fresh perspective might reveal a solution you hadn't considered.

2. Look around your living space and identify one activity that's become difficult; write down three alternative ways you might accomplish the same task, focusing on what's still possible rather than what's been lost.

3. Try approaching a daily challenge from a new angle today,

A good day thought: Write about a time that a different solution, something out of the ordinary made a difference.

The miracle isn't that the sun rises each morning, but that we're given the chance to rise with it, renewed.

itsgoingtobeagoodday©

19

The sounds of morning

Thomas stood frozen on the concrete path outside Willow Grove Senior Living, his mouth slightly open in wonder. There it was again—a sound he hadn't heard in decades. A melodic trill, high and clear, floating down from somewhere in the flowering dogwood tree that graced the community garden.

"Grandpa! What is it?" His granddaughter Rachel touched his arm gently, her eyes bright with concern.

He pointed upward, his hand trembling slightly. "A bird," he whispered, not wanting to scare it away. "I can hear a bird singing." The morning sun caught the tears gathering in his eyes, and Rachel squeezed his hand.

"That's what I've been trying to tell you!" She beamed at him. "These aren't like the clunky hearing aids you tried years ago. They're amazing now—they can even connect to your phone to stream music or answer questions, like having a tiny personal assistant right in your ear."

Thomas shook his head, still marveling at the clarity of the birdsong. "But Rachel, honey, you know I can't afford something like that. Not on my fixed income." He gestured at the modest senior living complex behind them. "I've made my peace with—"

"Stop right there," Rachel interrupted, guiding him to a nearby bench. "Medicare covers a big part of it now, and there are programs to help with the rest. I've already checked." She pulled out her tablet, showing him the information she'd gathered. "You deserve to hear everything, Grandpa.

The birds, your favorite country records, those terrible puns Mr. Rodriguez tells at the community coffee hour..."

Thomas chuckled despite himself. "They can't be that terrible if I haven't been able to hear them."

"Trust me," Rachel grinned, "they're awful. But you love them anyway."

As they sat there, the morning came alive around them. Thomas found himself turning his head at each new sound—the soft whir of Mrs. Helsel's electric scooter passing by, the distant church bells he hadn't heard in years, even the gentle splash of the community garden's small fountain.

"Listen to this," he said suddenly, his voice full of wonder. "Just listen!" He closed his eyes, taking it all in. "I can hear the wind in the leaves. I'd forgotten what that sounds like."

Rachel watched as her grandfather discovered each sound, his face lighting up like a child on Christmas morning. She pulled out her phone. "Want to try something really special? Remember how you always talked about that Patsy Cline concert you went to in '62?"

A few taps later, "Crazy" flowed through Thomas's hearing aids, and his hands flew to his mouth. The crystal-clear notes brought him right back to that night, to the warmth of the concert hall, to the magic of Patsy's voice. "Oh," was all he could manage.

A blue jay landed on the dogwood branch above them, adding its harsh call to the morning's symphony. Thomas laughed out loud. "Not exactly Patsy Cline, is it?"

"Well, you can't win them all," Rachel giggled. "But at least now you can hear Mr. Rodriguez tell his joke about the blue jay and the mailman."

"Do I want to?"

"Probably not. But I know you're going to laugh anyway."

Thomas put his arm around his granddaughter's shoulders, pulling her close. The morning air was filled with possibility—and better yet, he could hear every bit of it. From the chattering of squirrels in the garden to the cheerful "good mornings" of his neighbors heading to the community room for coffee, each sound was a gift being unwrapped.

"You know what the best part is?" he said softly.

"What's that?"

"I can finally hear you whisper 'I love you, Grandpa' without having to guess at the words."

Rachel's eyes grew watery. "I love you, Grandpa," she whispered.

"I know," he smiled. "I can hear you. Clear as a bell."

Above them, the dogwood tree burst into a chorus of morning birdsong, as if the birds were celebrating with them. Thomas closed his eyes again, letting the sounds wash over him. After so many years of muffled silence, the world had finally turned its volume back on—and it was playing him a symphony.

***

"The only constant is change," Heraclitus reminds us. This is a truth that becomes even more apparent as we age. We've seen firsthand how the world transforms. Just as people once resisted the change from horses to buggies, and from buggies to cars, we may find ourselves hesitant to embrace the new technologies and ways of life that constantly emerge. It's natural to feel comfortable with what we know.

"We often cling to the familiar, even when a better way appears. But progress, like time, marches on." (Anonymous)

"To resist change is to resist the future." (Proverb)

Perhaps today is the perfect day to open ourselves to something new. Even a small change, a slight shift in perspective, can reveal unexpected possibilities. It might just be the key to a brighter, more fulfilling day. It's going to be a good day.

*Inspired by my friends and coworkers who wear hearing aids.

***

It's Still Going to Be a Good Day!

We're all just figuring this life thing out, one day at a time. And a good day is always preferable to, not having a good day.

Three Things to Try Today to Make it a Good Day:

1. Listen to a favorite song from your youth and allow yourself to move to the music, even if just swaying in your chair or tapping your foot. I bet it makes you smile.

2. Watch birds or wildlife from your window for ten minutes, noticing their movements and behaviors.

3. Open your window for five minutes to let fresh air circulate, noticing the sounds and smells it brings.

The smallest act of kindness can cast light into someone's darkest hour—be generous with your sunshine.

20

It's going to be a good day: McKenna's race

The Arizona sun blazed overhead as five-year-old McKenna stood at the edge of the community pool, her tiny toes curling over the concrete lip. Her mother, Lisa, watched nervously from behind oversized sunglasses as the swimming instructor guided McKenna toward the water.

"Don't be scared," the instructor said, extending her hand.

McKenna tilted her head, confused. "I'm not scared." Without hesitation, she jumped in, disappearing beneath the surface before popping back up with a grin that revealed a missing front tooth.

After just twenty minutes, the instructor pulled Lisa aside. "Mrs. Jenkins, your daughter doesn't need swimming lessons. She's fearless in the water—goes straight to the bottom and comes right back up. What she needs is a swim team."

That evening, Lisa and her husband Mike discussed their daughter's apparent aquatic talent over dinner.

"A swim team?" Mike raised an eyebrow. "That's early mornings, weekends..."

"The instructor says she's got natural ability," Lisa replied.

The following week, they took McKenna to the local swim club. While other children clung to their parents, McKenna marched straight to the coach and introduced herself.

The drive home from that first practice was quiet until McKenna's small voice piped up from the backseat. "I'm going to be an Olympic swimmer," she announced with the certainty only a child could muster. "And nobody's going to stop me." Then she promptly fell asleep, dreams of blue ribbons dancing in her head.

Lisa and Mike exchanged knowing glances in the rearview mirror. Their daughter had found her element.

The years that followed were measured in laps and split times. Mike rose at 4:30 AM to drive McKenna to morning practice, thermos of coffee in hand. Lisa managed the logistics of meets, washing endless loads of chlorine-scented towels. Their weekends became a blur of humid indoor pools and stopwatches.

At McKenna's first real competition, Lisa watched her daughter line up with other six-year-olds, McKenna's shoulders barely reaching their elbows despite being the same age.

When the race ended and McKenna climbed out, Lisa rushed over. "Great job, sweetie! You did so well!"

McKenna's brow furrowed. "Were they racing?"

Lisa laughed. "Yes, it was a race."

"Oh." McKenna looked back at the pool thoughtfully. "If I'd known it was a race, I would've swam faster."

At the next meet, just before the starter's whistle, McKenna looked to the stands where her mother sat. Lisa mouthed clearly: "It's a race." McKenna nodded seriously, then dove in and left the competition in her wake.

They called her "Mini but Mighty" as she collected ribbons and medals, her bedroom walls gradually disappearing beneath them. One of her coaches, a former Olympic gold medalist, took special interest in McKenna's development.

"Swimming isn't just about winning," he'd tell her. "It's about discipline, resilience, and knowing that there's always another race."

***

Seventy-eight-year-old McKenna Jenkins adjusted her swim cap in the locker room mirror, the arthritis in her fingers making the simple task a struggle. The reflection showed a face mapped with laugh lines and eyes that still sparkled with determination.

Her days of competitive swimming were decades behind her. The medals were stored in boxes in her attic, the college scholarship had led to a fulfilling career as a physical therapist, and she'd raised three children who had all inherited her love of water.

She still swam every morning—slower now, but with the same joy she'd felt as a child. The pool had become her refuge after Mike passed away five years ago. The community center's "Silver Swimmers" group had become her second family.

Today was special, though. The center was hosting an intergenerational relay, pairing seniors with the current youth swim team. McKenna's partner was a shy twelve-year-old named Zoe who reminded her so much of herself.

"Ms. Jenkins?" Zoe approached, fidgeting with her goggles. "I'm nervous. What if I let the team down?"

McKenna smiled. "You know, Zoe, when I was about your age, I learned something important: there's always another race. Some days you win, some days you learn, but what matters is getting in the water."

Zoe nodded uncertainly.

"And one more thing," McKenna added with a wink. "It's a race."

They both laughed, and as they walked toward the pool deck, McKenna felt that familiar flutter of excitement. Her joints ached and her swimsuit didn't fit quite like it used to, but as she looked at the sparkling blue water, she knew with absolute certainty:

It was going to be a good day.

Because in swimming, as in life, it wasn't about how fast you went or how many medals you won. It was about finding joy in the journey, about getting up early and diving in even when the water seemed cold. It was about teaching the next generation that strength comes in all sizes, at all ages.

And most importantly, it was about remembering that no matter how old you get, there's always another race worth showing up for.

***

As McKenna's old coach used to say, "Life is like swimming a race. It's not about who finishes first, but about improving your own time and enjoying the journey through the water."

*Inspired by my niece McKenna and her coach.

***

Three Ways to Make Your Day a Good One:

1. **Set a Small, Achievable Goal** - Focus on the individual race or goal of the day, whatever it is. It could be as simple as walking to the mailbox, calling an old friend, or trying a new recipe.

2. **Find Your "Water"** - McKenna found peace and purpose in the pool throughout her life. Discover what activity brings you similar joy and make time for it today, whether it's gardening, music, art, or simply sitting outdoors.

3. **Practice "It's a Race" Mindfulness** - When facing a challenging task during the day, use McKenna's "it's a race" mantra as a form of mindful focus - being fully present for whatever you're doing and giving it your best effort, not to compete with others but to fully engage with life.

Memory keeps what matters, regardless of what time insists we forget

Mckenna

Your courage grows in the spaces between fear and wonder—make room for both today.

21

The tiny tech whisperer

The moment Gino and Amanda brought baby Ivy home from the hospital, they knew she was different from her sisters. Violet had been calm and observant, Rose artistic and dreamy. But Ivy—even as an infant—had a curious sparkle in her eyes that seemed to say, "Just you wait and see what I can do."

By eighteen months, Ivy had earned the family nickname "Hurricane." Not because she was destructive, but because wherever she went, things moved. Nothing was safe from her exploring hands and inquisitive mind. Child locks were mere suggestions. Baby gates were challenges to overcome.

"I swear she's going to be an engineer," Gino would say, watching Ivy methodically dismantle her stacking toys.

Amanda would laugh. "Or a master thief."

When Tutu Linda invited the family to her beachside home for the weekend, Amanda packed extra vigilantly. The beach house was a wonderland of potential dangers for a curious toddler: a swimming pool, stairs, shells small enough to swallow, and Tutu's prized collection of glass figurines.

"Are you sure we should bring her?" Amanda asked, folding tiny swimsuits and sundresses. "Maybe my sister could watch her for the weekend."

Gino looked up from where he was helping Rose and Violet pack their books. "Tutu's been asking to see her. Besides, between the four of us adults, we can keep an eye on one tiny hurricane."

But keeping track of Ivy proved more challenging than they anticipated. From the moment they arrived, she was in perpetual motion—reaching for shiny objects, attempting to climb the bookshelves, and trying to crawl under the deck to investigate a family of lizards.

"She's fearless," Tutu said, watching as Ivy determinedly climbed up on a chair, her little face focused with concentration.

"That's what worries me," Amanda replied, scooping her daughter up before she could reach the table. "She has no sense of danger."

On their second day at the beach house, they were invited to Tutu's neighbor's home for lunch. The Smiths had just built their house with all the latest technology—smart appliances, automated blinds, and an entertainment system that required three different remotes to operate.

"We'll put Ivy in the playpen while we eat," Amanda said, setting up the portable enclosure in the Smiths' living room. She placed Ivy inside with her favorite stuffed giraffe and a few board books.

The adults settled around the dining table in the next room, close enough to hear if Ivy fussed but far enough away for adult conversation. Mrs. Smith was showing off photos from their recent trip to Belize when Tutu suddenly tilted her head.

"Do you hear that?" she asked.

Everyone paused. The unmistakable sounds of a children's cartoon, floated from the living room.

"Did someone turn on the TV for Ivy?" Mr. Smith asked.

They all looked at each other and shook their heads.

Gino was the first to get up. The others followed, crowding in the doorway to an unexpected sight: Ivy was no longer in her playpen. Instead, she sat cross-legged on the couch, the large remote balanced carefully in her tiny hands, her eyes fixed on the colorful characters of Coco Melon singing about sharing on the enormous flat-screen television.

"How in the world...?" Mrs. Smith began.

"I didn't even know how to turn that system on," Mr. Smith admitted. "I have to use my sticky notes every time."

Ivy glanced up at her audience, gave a pleased grin, and returned her attention to the show.

Amanda approached carefully and sat beside her daughter. "Ivy, did you turn on the TV?"

Ivy nodded without looking away from the screen.

"How did she get out of the playpen?" Tutu whispered.

"More importantly, how did she figure out that complicated remote system?" Gino wondered.

They let her finish watching the show, mesmerized by the sight of this tiny person navigating technology that confounded most adults.

This wasn't a one-time occurrence. A week after returning home, Tutu called with a question.

"Check my Amazon account," she said. "There's a charge for a dancing unicorn toy that I didn't order."

After some investigation, they discovered that during their visit, Ivy had somehow gotten hold of Tutu's phone while she was napping, opened the Amazon app that was already logged in, and ordered herself a toy she had seen advertised on TV.

"She's not even two years old," Tutu said, equal parts impressed and concerned. "What will she be capable of by kindergarten?"

As months passed, Ivy's technological intuition only grew stronger. She could unlock smartphones, find her favorite apps, and navigate streaming services better than her grandmother. When the family got a voice-activated home system, Ivy was the first to master it, using it to play her favorite songs and turn the living room lights different colors.

One evening, as Gino struggled to pair his new smartwatch with his phone, Ivy toddled over, took the devices from his hands, and with a few seemingly random taps, completed the connection.

"Thank you," he said, stunned.

Ivy patted his hand. "S'easy, Daddy," she said, then wandered off to find her sisters.

Later that night, as Amanda and Gino prepared for bed, they reflected on their youngest daughter's unusual gift.

"You know," Amanda said, "watching Ivy makes me think I've been too quick to say 'I can't' when it comes to new technology."

Gino nodded. "We always joke about needing Rose to program the DVR or Violet to help with social media. But Ivy doesn't know she's not supposed to understand these things. She just... tries."

"No fear," Amanda agreed.

"Exactly like someone else I know," Gino smiled, taking her hand. "Remember how you taught yourself to rebuild a motorcycle engine when you were twenty-five?"

Amanda laughed. "I was too stubborn to ask for help and too broke to pay someone else."

"You were fearless," he said. "Just like our little hurricane."

The next day, when her new phone arrived, instead of asking one of the girls to set it up, Amanda sat down with the instructions. It took her twice as long as it would have taken Rose, but by dinner time, she had it configured exactly how she wanted it.

"Look at you," Tutu said during their weekly video call. "Next thing you know, you'll be teaching me how to use all these contraptions."

Amanda smiled, watching Ivy in the background carefully showing her cousin how to use the tablet they had given her for Christmas.

"It's never too late to learn something new," Amanda said. "If Ivy can do it before she can even tie her shoes, why can't we?"

Across the room, as if sensing she was being discussed, Ivy looked up and grinned, her eyes still holding that same sparkle that seemed to say, "Just you wait and see what I can do."

***

Anyone who stops learning is old, whether at twenty or eighty. Anyone who keeps learning stays young." - Henry Ford

Inspired by baby Ivy who really did turn the cartoons on the television while visiting, and also ordered a toy from Amazon.

***

Three Ways to Have a Good Day:

1. **Embrace the beginner's mind.** Approach new technology or challenges without preconceived notions of difficulty. Like Ivy, be curious rather than fearful when facing the unknown.

2. **Learn something new every day**. Set aside just fifteen minutes to explore a feature on your phone or computer you've never used before. Small steps lead to great journeys of discovery.

3. **Connect across generations through technology.** Reach out to someone older or younger and share your knowledge or ask for help. The exchange benefits everyone and builds meaningful bonds, just as Ivy and her great-grandmother connected through their tablet adventure.

***

Ivy

The most beautiful souls are those who've weathered storms yet still choose to dance in the rain.

22

A father's prayer

Sam watched the morning light filter through the blinds, casting thin golden lines across his coffee cup. It had been three months since Conrad called him with the good news—three months of cautious hope after years of desperate prayer.

"Dad," Conrad had said, his voice stronger than Sam had heard in nearly a decade, "I got the job. Full benefits. My own desk." Such simple things that most fathers took for granted from their sons, but to Sam, they were miracles.

Sam closed his eyes and remembered the first time he realized something was wrong. Conrad, barely fifteen, came home with bloodshot eyes and a strange, distant smile. "Just tired, Dad," he'd said, brushing past Sam to disappear into his room. The door locked with a decisive click.

By sixteen, Conrad had become a stranger in their home—a ghost who appeared briefly at odd hours, took food from the refrigerator, and vanished again. Hushed phone calls, unexplained absences from school, money missing from Sam's wallet. The classic signs that Sam had been too afraid to acknowledge.

"Lord," Sam whispered into his coffee, a prayer that had become as routine as breathing, "thank you for bringing him back to us."

The intervention had been a disaster. Conrad, then eighteen, had stormed out, screaming that they were trying to control him. "I don't have a problem! You're the ones with the problem!" The words still echoed in Sam's mind during sleepless nights.

For years after, Sam lived in fear of that phone call—the one every parent of an addict dreads. He'd see news reports of overdoses and feel his heart stop, imagining Conrad alone, cold, forgotten. He kept Conrad's childhood photo in his wallet, terrified that one day he'd need it to identify a body.

Sam's pastor had encouraged him to join a support group for parents of addicts. There, he learned he wasn't alone. Doctors, lawyers, teachers, laborers—addiction didn't discriminate. Their children were honor students, athletes, artists. Some of the most beautiful, promising young people, now trapped in a cycle they couldn't escape.

"Don't enable, but don't abandon," the group leader had advised. "Love them, but set boundaries. And pray. Never stop praying."

And Sam had prayed. Through the missed holidays. Through the manipulative phone calls asking for money. Through the brief, hopeful periods of sobriety that inevitably crumbled. Through the night Conrad appeared on his doorstep, skeletal and shaking, begging for help.

That night had been the turning point. "I'm tired, Dad," Conrad had whispered, looking suddenly like the little boy who used to climb into Sam's lap during thunderstorms. "I'm so tired of this life."

The halfway house hadn't been fancy—just a modest home where twelve men struggled daily with their demons. Sam visited every Sunday, watching as, slowly, his son's eyes cleared. Conrad began to speak about the future again. He attended meetings. He helped the newer residents. He called Sam just to talk about normal things—a movie he'd seen, a book he was reading.

One evening, as Sam was leaving after a visit, Conrad walked him to his car. "You know what I realized, Dad?" he'd said, looking up at the stars.

"I've missed so much. So many years just... gone." His voice broke. "But I'm still here. I still have time."

The coffee had grown cold in Sam's cup. He rose to pour it out, glancing at the clock. Conrad would be here in an hour for their weekly breakfast—a tradition they'd started after he completed the program. They'd go to the diner where Conrad would order the same thing every time—scrambled eggs, rye toast, black coffee. They'd talk about Conrad's job, his girlfriend, the small room he rented from a kind elderly couple.

Sometimes they'd talk about the hard stuff too—the cravings that still came, the amends Conrad was making, the therapy he attended. But mostly, they just enjoyed being father and son again.

Sam's phone buzzed with a text message.

Running a little early. See you in 30. Love you, Dad.

Sam smiled down at the screen. Yes, it was going to be a good day.

***

"Faith is taking the first step even when you don't see the whole staircase." - Martin Luther King Jr.

This story was inspired by my friend Woody, whose faith and perseverance and prayers helped guide his son back from addiction.

Three Good Things to Have a Good Day:

1. Hold hope close, even when darkness seems overwhelming—recovery is always possible.

2. Find strength in community—no one should face addiction's challenges alone.

3. Celebrate each small victory on the path to healing—they build the bridge to a brighter tomorrow.

Your heart is a compass that never fails—when in doubt, follow where kindness leads.

itsgoingtobeagoodday©

23

A second chance at forever

Tim stared at the empty dog bed in the corner of their new beachfront condo, the one that should have held Max. The move from their sprawling Ahwautukee home to Puerto Peñasco, Mexico had been planned as a grand adventure for all four of them—Tim, Mary, and their two beloved collies, Ranger and Max. But fate had other plans.

"He keeps looking for him," Mary whispered, watching as Ranger paced from room to room, nose to the ground, tracking a scent that was fading with each passing day. "I don't know how to tell him Max isn't coming back."

Their early retirement dream had materialized during the pandemic—escape the corporate rat race, sell the Arizona home, and relocate to the tranquil shores of the Sea of Cortez. Just weeks before the move, Max had crossed the rainbow bridge, leaving a hole in their hearts that seemed impossible to fill, especially for Ranger.

At night, Ranger would jump onto their bed—something he'd never done when Max was alive—and curl against Mary's side, his eyes reflecting a loneliness that mirrored their own.

Three months into their new life, Mary's phone pinged with a text message one morning as she sipped her coffee, the sound of waves crashing outside their window.

"Tim!" she gasped, nearly spilling her coffee. "Look at this!"

The text was from their neighbor Justine: "Saw this on Facebook and thought of you. Isn't this Max's twin?"

Tim peered over her shoulder at the attached photo. A collie, almost identical to Max, was up for adoption. The collie's rich wheat and honey colored fur with a white blaze between intelligent eyes was hauntingly familiar.

"It must be a sign," Mary whispered, her voice trembling with hope. "And it's in Puerto Peñasco! What are the odds?"

Tim immediately messaged the post. The response came quickly, but with unexpected news.

"I'm actually in Taos, New Mexico," the message read. "Must have posted to the wrong Puerto Peñasco group—there's a small town in New Mexico with the same name."

Mary's face fell. "New Mexico? That's a fifteen-hour drive."

Tim glanced at Ranger, who was staring at Max's photo on the mantle, his tail motionless.

"Maybe it's still meant to be," Tim said. "Let's make the trip. Ranger can meet him first—see if they connect."

Two days later, they found themselves in Taos, pulling up to a modest ranch house. The owner, Dave, greeted them with the collie on a leash.

"This is Harley," Dave said. "My father couldn't keep him—tried to train him as a herding dog on his farm, but Harley wasn't cut out for it."

Ranger, usually reserved with strangers, strained at his leash toward Harley. When they met nose to nose, both dogs froze, then began circling each other with increasing excitement.

"They act like they know each other," Dave remarked.

"You won't believe this," Tim said, "but Harley looks exactly like our Max who passed away before we moved to Mexico."

Dave's eyebrows shot up. "Mexico? Wait—you're in Puerto Peñasco? I have a condo there! Same complex as yours, based on your profile picture background."

Mary shook her head in disbelief. "The universe works in mysterious ways."

That night, with paperwork signed and Harley officially theirs, they stayed at a pet-friendly hotel. Ranger, who hadn't left Harley's side since their introduction, guided the newcomer to the bed. For the first time since Max's passing, Ranger didn't sleep pressed against Mary—instead, he made room between them for Harley.

When they returned to Puerto Peñasco, something magical happened. Ranger's melancholy lifted. Occasionally, they'd catch him staring at Max's photo on the mantle, but now Harley would pad over, nudge Ranger's shoulder, as if to say, "I'm here now. It's okay."

"Do you think..." Mary started one evening as they watched both collies racing along the shoreline.

"That Harley somehow carries Max's spirit?" Tim finished her thought. "I don't know. But I do know that love doesn't just disappear. It finds new ways to express itself."

Their neighbor Justine visited a week later, marveling at their new addition. "He's beautiful! You know, if you want to help more dogs, there's Barb's Dog Rescue just outside town. Started by an American woman who lost her daughter to a drunk driver. The daughter loved rescuing dogs, so Barb created this sanctuary in her memory."

The following weekend, Tim and Mary visited Barb's Dog Rescue. The sight of hundreds of dogs—all shapes, sizes, and stories—moved them deeply.

"We can't adopt another right now," Mary told Barb, a strong-willed woman with kind eyes, "but we'd love to help."

They brought treats for the dogs and coffee for the volunteers. They shared success stories online that led to more adoptions.

On the anniversary of Max's passing, they sat on their balcony watching Ranger and Harley sleeping side by side, paws touching.

"Loss led us here," Tim reflected, "but look at how much love came from it."

Mary nodded, thinking of Max, and of all the dogs that come and go in your life. "Sometimes," she said, "the hardest goodbye leads to the most beautiful hello."

Down on the beach, a stray dog approached their condo, drawn by some unseen force. Tomorrow, they would bring her to Barb's. Another chance at forever, continuing the circle of rescue, healing, and love.

As Roger Caras once said, "Dogs are not our whole life, but they make our lives whole." For Tim and Mary, this truth had never resonated more deeply than now.

Inspired by Tim and Mary Coghlin and Max, Ranger and Harley.

***

To make it a good day:

1. **Rescue an animal**—you save two lives: the one you adopt and the space you create for another.

2. **Volunteer your time**—even an hour makes a difference to creatures waiting for human connection.

3. **Share a rescue story**—inspiration spreads, creating ripples of compassion that reach farther than you know.

Some hearts are lighthouses
—they don't need to move
to guide others home.

Max and
Ranger

Harley and
Ranger

The light you're searching for has always lived within you—sometimes it just needs your permission to shine

itsgoingtobeagoodday©

24

Refusing to fall: A stuntman's true story

Arizona, 1975. The desert sun beat down on Washington High's outdoor pool in Phoenix as Steve Silver stood at the edge of the high diving board, his crutch discarded at the ladder's base. The gathered crowd fell silent. Some looked away, uncomfortable. Others stared with morbid curiosity. No one believed he would jump.

No one except Tommy Rodriguez, Steve's best friend since third grade.

"You got this, Silver!" Tommy shouted, his voice echoing across the water.

Steve didn't look down. Not at the water, not at his missing right leg—amputated six months earlier after a devastating cancer diagnosis during his junior year. He simply focused on the horizon, took a deep breath, and leapt.

The perfect arc. The clean entry. The eruption of cheers as he surfaced, grinning.

That was Steve Silver. Seventeen years old and already refusing to be defined by what he'd lost.

***

"You're out of your mind," Tommy said, leaning against Steve's souped-up 1968 Camaro. "California? Hollywood? Stuntmen need two legs, man."

Steve tightened the last bolt on his custom-rigged clutch system and slid out from under the car. "Says who?"

"Says everyone! That's like... physics or something."

Steve wiped grease from his hands. "Yeah, well, 'everyone' said I wouldn't walk again. 'Everyone' said I should get a desk job. 'Everyone' can kiss my one-legged ass."

Tommy laughed despite himself. "Your funeral, Silver."

Two days after graduation, Steve packed his few belongings into the Camaro. His parents stood in the driveway, his mother crying, his father trying not to.

"I'll call when I get there," Steve promised.

His father pressed an envelope into his hand. "Gas money," he said gruffly. "And a little extra. Just in case."

As Phoenix disappeared in his rearview mirror, Steve felt something he hadn't experienced since before the cancer: absolute freedom.

***

Los Angeles, 1976. Steve's hundredth rejection.

"Look, kid, I admire your... spirit." The stunt coordinator—Bobby Jenkins, a legend in the industry—looked genuinely uncomfortable. "But this isn't some after-school special. People die doing this work. With your... condition..."

"It's not a condition," Steve interrupted. "It's an amputation. And it doesn't affect my driving, my climbing, or my falling. I can do everything your guys can do. Some things better."

Jenkins sighed. "Show me."

Steve had prepared for this moment. He executed a perfect fall, rolled, and came up standing on his prosthetic leg. He demonstrated a controlled tumble down a short flight of stairs. He showed off the custom modifications he'd made to his prosthetic for different stunts.

Jenkins watched, arms crossed, expression unreadable. When Steve finished, sweating but standing tall, the older man simply nodded.

"Be at Paramount tomorrow. Six AM. You're coffee boy until I say otherwise."

It wasn't a stunt job. It wasn't even a real job. But it was a foot in the door—a reality that made Steve chuckle darkly as he drove back to his tiny apartment.

"Coffee boy" became "that one-legged kid who hangs around" became "Silver" became "the guy who fixed the rig when Johnson couldn't" became "the crazy one who jumped when no one else would."

Small jobs. Dangerous jobs. Jobs no one wanted. Steve took them all, performing each with a precision born of knowing he couldn't afford to fail. Not even once.

He lived on ramen and determination, sending half his meager earnings back to his parents in Phoenix. The other half went to better prosthetics, physical therapy, and keeping his beloved Camaro running.

By 1980, Steve Silver was no longer a novelty act. He was a professional with a growing reputation for taking on the impossible without complaint.

The day Chuck Norris walked onto the set of "Invasion U.S.A.," Steve was rigging a car for a controlled crash sequence.

"You Silver?" Norris asked, squinting against theCalifornia sun.

Steve straightened, wiping his hands on his jeans."Yes, sir."

"They tell me you're the best driver on the crew."

"I get by."

Norris' eyes flicked briefly to Steve's prosthetic leg, then back to his face. "They also tell me you've been practicing martial arts."

Steve shrugged. "Helps with balance. Coordination."

"Show me."

There, in the dusty back lot, Steve demonstrated the moves he'd been practicing in private for months. His movements weren't as fluid as they could be—would never be—but they were precise, controlled, and powerful.

When he finished, Norris nodded. "I need someone who can drive through an exploding building, take a hit, and make it look good. You interested?"

Steve didn't hesitate. "When do we start?"

***

Steve's mother kept a scrapbook. Newspaper clippings. Magazine interviews. Movie posters with her son's name in tiny print under "Stunt Coordinator."

His favorite was a Polaroid taken on the set of "Delta Force 2." In it, Steve stood beside Chuck Norris, both men grinning, dusty and exhausted after a complex action sequence. On the back, Norris had scrawled: "To Steve—the only man I know who can do more with one leg than most can do with two."

Steve Silver never became famous, not in the way actors did. But in Hollywood's tight-knit stunt community, he became legendary—not as the one-legged stuntman, but simply as one of the best in the business.

On rare visits home to Phoenix, neighborhood kids would gather around as he worked on his Camaro, peppering him with questions about Hollywood and famous actors.

"Is it hard," one bold youngster finally asked, "doing all that with just one leg?"

Steve looked up from the engine, considering the question seriously.

"The hardest part," he said finally, "was convincing everyone else it wasn't impossible." He grinned. "The rest was just physics—and stubbornness."

As the desert sun set behind the mountains, painting the sky in shades of orange and purple, Steve Silver leaned against his car and realized he'd traveled much further than the 400 miles between Phoenix and Los Angeles.

He'd come all the way from "I can't" to "I did."

"A hero is an ordinary individual who finds the strength to persevere and endure in spite of overwhelming obstacles." – Christopher Reeve

Inspired by my husbands high school friend, stuntman Steve Solo, known for Colors (1988), Invasion U.S.A. (1985), and Delta Force 2: The Colombian Connection (1990).

***

Three Suggestions for Having a Good Day (Inspired by the Story)

1. **Adapt Rather Than Surrender** – Just as Steve modified his car and prosthetic to achieve what others thought impossible, find creative solutions to your challenges rather than giving up. As Jimmy Dean said, "I can't change the direction of the wind, but I can adjust my sails to always reach my destination."

2. **Focus on Possibilities, Not Limitations** – Steve concentrated on what he could do exceptionally well rather than dwelling on what he couldn't do. Stephen Hawking advised: "Concentrate on things your disability doesn't prevent you doing well, and don't regret the things it interferes with."

3. **Challenge Expectations** – Steve's greatest triumphs came when he did what others said was impossible. Each day, look for one expectation to defy or one boundary to push.

"Dost thou love life? Then do not squander time; for that's the stuff life is made of." - Benjamin Franklin

Perhaps the truest wealth is measured in moments we'd never trade for anything money could buy.

25

Not all about the money

The last time Anita saw her father alive, he asked her to get his wallet from the hospital room drawer.

"Dad, I don't need your money," she said, glancing at her phone where three urgent work emails demanded her attention.

"Just get my wallet." His voice was soft but firm, the same tone he'd used when she was a little girl refusing to eat her vegetables.

Anita sighed and retrieved the worn leather billfold. The hospital lighting made everything look harsh and clinical, but the wallet seemed warm in her hands, shaped by decades of sitting in her father's back pocket. Inside just a twenty-dollar bill, a few ones, a faded driver's license and a photo of her mother from twenty years ago.

"What do you need, Dad?" She checked her watch. The conference call about the million-dollar hospital contract was in forty minutes, and she still needed to review the terms.

He patted the bed beside him. Reluctantly, she sat down, feeling the starched hospital sheet beneath her fingertips.

"Do you see this, baby girl?" He held up the wallet with trembling hands. "It's not all about the money."

"Yeah, I know that, Dad."

"Do you?" His eyes—hazel and still with a twinkle of mischief—studied her face. "You're my youngest of six, working that stressful job. Not married, no children. I know you own your house, have a nice car but I just wonder if you really know that it's not all about the money."

Anita stiffened. "I have a good life. I'm happy Dad—"

"Your mother and I married young. Had six children." He closed the wallet, clutching it in hands mapped with veins and liver spots. "The life we lived? It was definitely not about the money."

She thought about her childhood—the crowded dinner table, the hand-me-downs, the road trips and weekends at the hunting camp instead of resort vacations. But there had been laughter, always laughter and always love.

Her father shifted in bed, grimacing. The absence below his knees was still jarring to her. She adjusted the beautiful quilt someone had made and dropped off, so it went to the end of the bed. A hunter and fisherman all his life, now with both legs amputated due to complications from diabetes. Unfathomable.

"You should fly back to Arizona," he said suddenly. "You're going to need to take more time off when I start physical therapy. To help your mother."

"Dad, I can stay—"

"No, you leave. Go home, Anita. Rest. Come back fresh and be there for your mother."

Something in his tone made her comply. She kissed his forehead, inhaling the familiar scent that persisted beneath the antiseptic hospital smell. "I'll be back in a few weeks."

"I love you, baby girl."

"Love you too, Dad."

When Anita landed in Phoenix at 11:00 PM, her suitcase still packed from Pittsburgh, she felt a strange hollowness. Her house seemed too big, too quiet. She wandered through the rooms with their carefully selected furniture and artwork, trying to find space in her mind for the worry about her mother, the stress about her father, and for what had happened in such a short time.

The phone rang.

She knew before answering. Some primal part of her recognized the specific cadence of a late-night ring bearing bad news.

Her father was gone.

As her sister's tearful voice confirmed what she already knew, Anita sank to the floor beside her unpacked suitcase. Maybe he had known. Maybe he hadn't wanted her to be there when he took his last breath.

The week after the funeral passed in a blur of arrangements and relatives. Anita's corporate office had sent flowers but emails continued to pile up. A million-dollar contract waited for no one's grief.

In her mother's bedroom, Anita watched as her mother methodically folded up her father's favorite flannel shirt.

"He was proud of you," her mother said quietly. "But he worried."

"About money? I'm doing fine, Mom."

"Not about money. About joy." Her mother's hands stilled on the mug. "He always said you were the one who couldn't settle. Stubborn. Driven." She smiled sadly. "He didn't want you to learn the hard way, that some things can't be bought. Time. Chances."

That night, in her childhood bedroom, Anita found an old notebook. Inside, in her teenage handwriting: Someday I'll write stories that change people's lives.

She remembered telling her father about this dream, sitting on their front porch under a Pennsylvania moon. He had nodded and said, "You'll do it, too. When you're ready to put down all those other things you're carrying."

Three weeks later, Anita gave notice at her corporate job. Not for a competitor. Not for a better salary. Her colleagues were bewildered.

"I'm moving to the water in Mexico," she told her boss. "A small beach village on the Sea of Cortez. Puerto Penasco."

"To do what?" she asked, genuinely confused.

Anita smiled. "To write my book."

She sold her house, sold the car, sold the hot tub. Kept only what would fit in for her next life.

Life changes in an instant. Someone is here one day and gone the next. A decision can change your life forever.

If she hadn't moved to Puerto Penasco, Anita would never have met Diego, with his kind brown eyes and quiet laughter, on a sailboat on the Sea of Cortez. She wouldn't have written her first book sitting on a balcony overlooking the water, the same water that brought in the beautiful tides on her barefoot beach wedding.

Diego, who after their first date, told her to follow her dreams with or without him. A man who read her pages of her novel each morning. "Your father," he asked once, "he gave you good advice?"

"The best," Anita replied, watching the sunset paint the water orange and red. "It just took me a while to hear it."

Sometimes it's just one piece of advice, those words from someone who has lived their whole life—seventy-seven years of learning—that can set the wheel in motion. Words that change your life forever, if only you're ready to listen.

Anita touched the small, worn wallet she now kept in her desk drawer. Inside was her father's driver's license photo, his kind eyes still visible, and a single note written in her hand:

It's not all about the money.

***

To laugh often and much; to win the respect of intelligent people and the affection of children... to leave the world a bit better... to know even one life has breathed easier because you have lived. This is to have succeeded."
Ralph Waldo Emerson (1841)

"For my father. Our last day together, he asked me to get his wallet and told me, 'It's not all about the money, baby girl.'" In case you are reading this...I listened Dad.

Three Suggestions for Having a Good Day

1. Ask a family member to teach you something they know how to do that you've never learned, no matter how simple it might seem.

2. Try holding your fork or spoon in your non-dominant hand during one meal, awakening your brain with this simple change in routine.

3. Reach out to someone younger or older than you and ask what brings them joy these days—their answer might introduce you to something new worth trying.

Perhaps we are all just walking each other home, one gentle moment at a time.

🎉 KINDNESS CONFETTI ALERT! 🎉
SCAN NOW & RECEIVE KINDNESS BONUS! 📱✨
Want to sprinkle kindness around like confetti?
💐 FREE PRINTABLE KINDNESS CARDS 💐 Just for YOU!

I hope this little book brought a spark of light to your day today. If it did, it would truly make my day if you'd take a moment to share your thoughts wherever you found this book. I read and cherish my readers' words. Remember, the best days often come from the kindness of others - so maybe pass this book along to someone who could use a gentle reminder that they can handle whatever comes their way.

26

A note from the author

In writing this book, I experienced an ironic twist of fate when "It's Going to Be a Good Day" was completely lost with all its final edits due to a new writing program. Yet somehow, I managed to recover the majority of it. How could I possibly be upset at a book called "It's Going to Be a Good Day"? So as the title suggests—it is, indeed, going to be a good day. And here it is, whether you're experiencing these stories in print, ebook, or audio.

Thank you for taking this journey with me. I hope at least one of these stories resonated with you and created a small spark of difference in your everyday life. Sometimes we just need to pause and consider our own circumstances in relation to others—to take a moment to breathe, to reflect.

All these stories are inspired by real people and true events, although most names have been fictionalized and a few details added for storytelling purposes. I'm deeply grateful to everyone who shared their experiences and allowed me to transform them into these narratives. Special thanks to my cousin Adam Thomas, who actually wrote his story instead of telling it to me—it was simply too good for me to rewrite.

My heartfelt appreciation goes to my friends and family who patiently endured my relentless questioning whenever we gathered, as I searched for stories worth sharing. I know I can be persistent, and I thank you for your grace.

***

May these pages remind you that even in life's ordinary moments, there's something extraordinary waiting to be discovered.

***

Anita loves connecting with readers like you. Reach out anytime at hello @aksmithauthor.com with your thoughts or experiences. Whether you've tucked this book beside your bed, kept it as a bathroom companion for quiet moments of reflection, gifted it to someone needing encouragement, or found comfort in its pages during a hospital stay, your experience matters. If these stories touched your heart, a brief Amazon review would be the greatest gift you could give in return—it helps these stories find their way to others who might need them too. Thank you for being part of this journey. And remember, It's going to be a good day!

Anita Kaltenbaugh writes to encourage kindness, inspiration, and grace in everyday life. This collection of stories blossomed from her desire to offer comfort and wisdom to her mother and friends during challenging times, only to discover she had an abundance of tales that transform ordinary moments into life lessons.

When not writing under her own name, Anita creates as A.K. Smith, having penned two acclaimed suspense novels: the award-winning "A Deep Thing" and "Her Perfect Disappearance." Her creative spirit also brings joy to younger readers through her children's picture book series, "The Sparkling Adventures of Glowy the Fish," set in the enchanting Sea of Cortez.

Dividing her time between Arizona and a tiny beach island in Mexico, Anita finds endless inspiration in the rhythm of the sea and the warmth of the local community. Her Pennsylvania roots and southwestern life have gifted her a unique perspective on the beautiful complexity of human experience.

If you find yourself thinking of a story about life's ordinary moments that might inspire someone, Anita welcomes your ideas at info@book swithsoul.com. You need only share the seed of inspiration—Anita will nurture it into a story and would be delighted to connect with you should your idea bloom in a future collection.

Remember, the best way to make it a good day for any author is to give a thumbs up on Amazon, or write a one to two sentence review on Goodreads, Amazon or wherever you purchased it! It really does matter to us!

Anita Kaltenbaugh writes suspense novels
and children's picture books
under the pen name

A.K. Smith

Suspense for Adults

A Deep Thing
Her Perfect Disappearance

Children's Books

The Sparkling Adventures of Glowy the Fish
Glowy's Great Escape
Glowy and the Lost Treasure
Glowy and the Misunderstood Shark
Glowy meets Crabby Patty
Glowy and Spotty Scotty
Glowy and the Mermaid who loves sparkles

www.aksmithauthor.com

www.ingramcontent.com/pod-product-compliance
Lightning Source LLC
Chambersburg PA
CBHW051308120626
46547CB00015B/2143